NOTHING BUT THE TRUTH

THE TRUTH AND
NOTHING BUT
THE TRUTH

JOHN F MACARTHUR, JR

CHRISTIAN FOCUS PUBLICATIONS

But in your hearts set apart Christ as Lord.
Always be prepared to give an answer to everyone who
asks you to give the reason for the hope that you have.

1 Peter 3:15

CONTENTS

Introduction   9

Part I: The Attitude for Evangelism

1 *The Christian's Duty in a Hostile World*   15

2 *Our Testimony as Salt and Light*   25

3 *Praying for the Lost*   35

Part II: What We Proclaim and Defend

4 *Who Is God?*   49

5 *The Reliability of Scripture*   63

6 *Amazing Prophecies*   77

7 *The Reality of Sin*   89

8 *The Virgin Birth and Deity of Jesus Christ*   101

9 *The Death and Resurrection of Jesus Christ*   115

Part III: Taking It to the Streets

10 *The Great Commission*   133

11 *How to Witness*   147

Appendix: "Who Do You Say That I Am?"   165

Study Guide   171

Scripture Index   193

General Index   201

INTRODUCTION

Being a witness to the Gospel in our day and age is becoming increasingly difficult. As the world rushes into and enters a new millennium, evangelical Christianity has reached a crossroads, especially here in the United States. After being influenced for some 150 years with strong biblical Christianity, our country has been rapidly declining, especially during the last half of the twentieth century and moving into the twenty-first. Practical atheism and moral relativism have dominated our society in recent decades. For the most part the few vestiges of Christianity still reflected in our culture are weak and compromising. Although many parts of our culture still wear some sort of religious mask, in reality it is largely pagan.

For a brief period, the spiritual revival of the 1970s that swept across the campuses of many colleges and universities seemed to promise a new day of blessing. Mass baptisms were conducted in rivers, lakes, and the ocean. Several new versions of the English Bible were released. Christian publishing and broadcasting experienced remarkable growth. Certainly an undeniable wind of the Spirit was blowing.

But that evangelical revival soon slowed and was overshadowed by the greed and debauchery of the eighties and nineties. From government leaders and celebrities right on down to average people, much of society became openly disparaging of biblical standards of morality and of Christianity as a whole. As a result, America adopted not only a non-Christian but a distinctly anti-Christian stance and agenda, with the state often encroaching on religious freedoms, instituting policies that are blatantly anti-Christian.

Understandably, evangelicals became resentful of this secular trend, appalled that biblical standards of ethics could be so blatantly rejected while vulgarity, profanity, and blasphemy were not only condoned but admired. In reaction, many well-meaning Christian leaders founded organizations to counteract such anti-Christian inroads. They declared war on the prevailing secular culture, especially on the liberal national media. This culture war has been essentially an effort to moralize the unconverted. But the end result of such an approach is that many Christians became hostile to unbelievers—the very ones God called them to love and reach with the Gospel.

At the beginning of 1999, a major battle in the culture war took place. The Bill Clinton impeachment hearings, conducted by the highest level of leadership in our nation, were in reality a referendum on the culture war. But what began as outrage against immorality, deception, and abuse of power ended rather abruptly without any punishment or even censure.

May I suggest that the culture war, at least as we know it, is now over. The impeachment process gave us a clear indication of where our culture stands—and we have discovered that it refuses to follow a biblical morality. The culture war is over—and we've lost. That was the inevitable end because this world is the domain of darkness, whether it's portrayed as moral or immoral. Our responsibility has never been to moralize the unconverted; it's to convert the immoral. Our responsibility is redemptive, not political. We do not have a moral agenda; we have a redemptive agenda. We can't reform the kingdom of darkness that Satan rules.

The cause of Christ cannot be protected or expanded by social intimidation any more than by government decree or military conquest. Ours is a spiritual warfare against human ideologies and beliefs that are set up against God, and those can be successfully conquered only with the weapon of the Word of God (see 2 Cor. 10:3-5). We can change society only by faithfully proclaiming the Gospel, which changes lives from the inside out.

The single divine calling of the church is to bring sinful people to salvation through Christ. If we do not lead the lost to salvation, nothing else we do for them, no matter how beneficial at the time, is of any eternal consequence. How to go about doing that is what this book is about.

In the first century, Christians faced a much more antagonistic culture than ours. They lived in a world of murderous tyrants, gross inequality and injustice, and sexual looseness and perversion. The apostle Peter knew how difficult it was for believers, especially new converts who were being persecuted for their faith, to face such a culture. That's why he described them as "aliens and strangers" (1 Pet. 2:11). They were like foreigners living without a permanent home or citizenship. That is also our standing, and we need to have that perspective when interacting with a culture that will become increasingly hostile to our faith.

To encourage all believers in such circumstances, Peter wrote, "Keep your behavior excellent among the [unsaved], so that . . . they may on account of your good deeds, as they observe them, glorify God in the day of visitation" (v. 12), and so "by doing right you may silence the ignorance of foolish men" (v. 15). We silence our adversaries by disproving their accusations and doing right—by living godly lives. That's our most effective tool for evangelism. Scandalous conduct fuels the fires of criticism, but godly living extinguishes them.

But along with that, Peter also encourages believers to always be "ready to make a defense to every one who asks you to give an account for the hope that is in you, yet with gentleness and reverence" (1 Pet. 3:15). When society attacks, we need to be prepared to "make a defense."

The Greek term translated "defense" often speaks of a formal defense in a court of law. But the apostle Paul also used the word in the informal sense of being able to answer anyone who questioned him (Phil. 1:16-17)—not just a judge, magistrate, or governor. Furthermore, "always" in 1 Peter 3:15 indicates that a believer should be prepared to answer in all situations, not just in the legal sphere.

So Peter's use of "defense" is general. Whether formally in an official setting or informally to anyone who might inquire, we must be ready to provide an answer about "the hope that is in [us]." And that hope refers to the Christian faith. Thus we should be able to give a rational explanation of our salvation and Christian faith.

We are to explain our faith "with gentleness and reverence." We should maintain a tender and gracious attitude in speaking. "Gentleness" speaks of meekness or humility and refers to power under control. "Reverence" refers to a kind of fear that involves a healthy devotion to God, a healthy regard for truth, and a healthy respect for the person being spoken to.

When a witness takes the stand in an American courtroom, he is asked to tell "the truth, the whole truth, and nothing but the truth." Similarly, believers in this evil culture must bear witness to God's truth. My goal in this book is to show you how to do that—how to uphold our precious Gospel in the midst of this doubting age.

The first part will discuss the attitude and preparedness we need to have before we can communicate our faith. You will learn how to live effectively in our hostile world, how to live as salt and light, and how to pray for the lost.

The second part will then focus on the major themes that are essential to our proclamation and defense of the faith. I have included chapters on God, Scripture, sin, and the deity, death, and resurrection of Christ. Those are the crucial elements of our faith—what we need to know and be certain of in order to be effective witnesses to the lost.

In the final section you'll learn how to take what we've studied to the streets, as it were. Here we'll examine our priority to be obedient to Christ's command to go and make disciples. We'll also take a practical look at how to be effective in witnessing for Christ. Finally, I will provide you a sample gospel presentation you can use in your evangelism efforts.

We are living in unprecedented times. The time of Christ's return is closer now than it has ever been. May you become a champion for His truth, His whole truth, and nothing but His truth in our doubting world.

PART ONE

THE

ATTITUDE

FOR

EVANGELISM

Chapter 1

THE CHRISTIAN'S DUTY IN A HOSTILE WORLD

As today's world makes the transition to living in the twenty-first century, many people still have as one of their mottos, "The more things change, the more they stay the same." Although there is an element of truth in that adage, we need to understand that many things are changing much faster than we may have realized and that man's sinfulness is more acute than ever (2 Tim. 3:13). The spiralling downward described in Romans 1:18-32 has occurred in our culture and we have reached the lowest level—"the reprobate mind." The Great Commission (Matt. 28:18-20), however, remains unchanged, as does the truth of our Lord's words, "The harvest is plentiful, but the workers are few. Therefore beseech the Lord of the harvest to send out workers into His harvest" (9:37-38).

But the church's focus on Christ's commands to evangelize has become more and more blurry, and many professing believers have not been faithful in witnessing to a hostile world. Instead, many believers' attitudes have increasingly reflected those of some of the churches in Asia Minor, including the one in Ephesus, to whom Christ said, "But I have this against you, that you have left your first love" (Rev. 2:4). He also severely admonished the church in Laodicea, "I know your deeds, that you are neither cold nor hot; I would that you were cold or hot. So because you are lukewarm, and neither hot nor cold, I will spit you out of My mouth" (3:15-16). As a fast-changing society becomes more hostile and more sinful, and as the church becomes weaker and more *like* the world rather than *distinct from* the world, we could well adopt this revised slogan: "The more things in the world change, the more intently and urgently we need to proclaim the unchanging truths of the Gospel to the unsaved."

THE CHURCH'S GREAT NEED

What then does the church, and all who profess membership in it, need in order to be faithful to the God-given mandate of evangelism? The answer is, a spiritual revival and renewal in which individual believers, enabled, freshly motivated, and reenergized by the Holy Spirit, focus their attention on the glory and majesty of God, and out of love for and delight in Him eagerly fulfill their spiritual duties and conscientiously follow the divine blueprint for the church. This means reversing the trends that have made the evangelical church a popularized institution that continues to eliminate every offense from its message. It means not ministering on the basis of pragmatism, psychology, or simply what feels right but rather according to biblical principles. It means opposing the trend toward a "seeker sensitive" ministry that employs all the most useful secular marketing strategies in attempting to reach the "felt needs" of today's culture, and, thereby, affirms the culture.

The contemporary church has grown content with a user-friendly, problem-solving approach that allows people to remain in their comfort zones without seriously being challenged to live righteously. Such an environment encourages "easy believism" (the view that says becoming a Christian is "easy"—simply give mental assent to who Jesus was and what He did for you, and don't necessarily be concerned about repentance from sin or obedience to Christ). Therefore many men and women who identify themselves as evangelical Christians are not really believers at all. They know little or nothing of God-honoring worship, holy aspirations, biblical obedience, or careful expository preaching, and have little expectancy for the Christian's future hope, which is the return of Jesus Christ. Absent is the Christ-centered faith and God-centered life that enable us to endure the difficulties and opposition of a hostile world and proclaim the Gospel effectively to it.

THE BELIEVER'S INCENTIVE

One of the ways the church can recapture a zeal for evangelism is by a serious focus on the reality of Christ's return—one that fosters an expectancy that at any moment of any day we could "be caught up . . . in the clouds to meet the Lord in the air, and so we shall always be with the Lord" (1 Thess. 4:17). Prominent church leaders throughout history have had a profound sense of awe and expectancy when contemplating Jesus' second coming. Here is what John Newton (author of "Amazing Grace") wrote in the first two verses of a 1774 hymn:

> *Day of judgment! day of wonders!*
> *Hark! The trumpet's awful sound,*
> *Louder than a thousand thunders,*
> *Shakes the vast creation round.*
> *How the summons will the sinner's*
>   *heart confound!*
>
> *See the Judge, our nature wearing,*
> *Clothed in majesty divine;*
> *You who long for his appearing*
> *Then shall say, This God is mine!*
> *Gracious Saviour, own me in that day as thine.*

The apostle Peter, in his first letter to believers in Asia Minor who were struggling to live for Christ in the midst of much persecution, reminds them and us that the end of the age and the glorious return of Christ are imminent. Peter then uses the incentive of that twofold truth to exhort believers to live faithfully, no matter how difficult the circumstances: "The end of all things is at hand; therefore, be of sound judgment and sober spirit for the purpose of prayer. Above all, keep fervent in your love for one another, because love covers a multitude of sins" (4:7-8).

The End Times Are Already Here

For members of the early church, such as Peter's audience, who were scattered around the Mediterranean world in the first century, the realization was emerging that, since the arrival of Messiah, they had already entered the last days. In addition to Peter's assertion, other Spirit-inspired New Testament letters make that fact clear. The apostle Paul stated such when he warned Timothy with a detailed description of the apostates who were then beginning to threaten the church: "But realize this, that in the last days difficult times will come. For men will be lovers of self, lovers of money, boastful, arrogant, revilers, disobedient to parents, ungrateful, unholy, unloving, irreconcilable, malicious gossips, without self-control, brutal, haters of good, treacherous, reckless, conceited, lovers of pleasure rather than lovers of God, holding to a form of godliness, although they have denied its power; and avoid such men as these" (2 Tim. 3:1-5; cf. 1 Tim. 4:1). The apostle John told his readers, "Children, it is the last hour; and just as you heard that antichrist is coming, even now many antichrists have arisen; from this we know that it is the last hour" (1 John 2:18).

The more astute Jewish Christians in the early church also would have known that technically the last days began with Christ's first coming because His coming marked the fulfillment of the Abrahamic Covenant and the ratification of the New Covenant, the key to God's plan of redemption. The Lord's death, which ratified the New Covenant, necessarily signified the end of the Jewish sacrificial system. The Old Testament system of priests, rituals, sacrifices, and offerings was swept away when the Lord Jesus offered the full and final sacrifice for sin and all believers became priests with access to God. This privilege was symbolized when the temple veil between the Holy Place and the Holy of Holies was miraculously torn in two from top to bottom (Matt. 27:51; Heb. 10:14-22; cf. Matt. 24:2; Heb. 9:26-28).

The Imminence of the Second Coming

When Peter wrote of "the end" (Greek, *telos*) being near (1 Pet. 4:7), he was not just referring to a cessation or to chronological termination. The word actually means consummation, an objective that is fulfilled or attained. In this context the apostle is alluding to the return of Jesus Christ when "all things" will be consummated. Earlier in the epistle, the apostle refers to this great event when he assures Christians they are protected by God's power "for a salvation ready to be revealed in the last time" (1:5), "at the revelation of Jesus Christ" (v. 7).

Peter identifies the climax of history as being "at hand" (1 Pet. 4:7). The Greek verb tense denotes a process consummated, with a resulting nearness. In this case it means Christ's return is imminent, which implies that believers should live and minister with expectancy because the Lord's Second Coming could occur at any moment. Such an attitude is a sign of faithfulness, as various New Testament passages underscore.

An eagerness for Christ's return was part of the good report Paul received about the church in Thessalonica: "For they themselves report about us what kind of a reception we had with you, and how you turned to God from idols to serve a living and true God, and to wait for His Son from heaven, whom He raised from the dead, that is Jesus, who delivers us from the wrath to come" (1 Thess. 1:9-10).

James encouraged believers to persevere in light of the certainty that Christ could return sooner than they realized: "Be patient, therefore, brethren, until the coming of the Lord. Behold, the farmer waits for the precious produce of the soil, being patient about it, until it gets the early and late rains. You too be patient; strengthen your hearts, for the coming of the Lord is at hand" (Jas. 5:7-8). The expression "is at hand" reminds us again that Jesus' coming for the church is to be anticipated by all believers in every age. That reality ought to be the focus of our hearts and minds as we serve Him daily. Just because He did not return during James' time does not invalidate the apostle's exhortation to the early Christians or to us.

God in His sovereign wisdom has chosen not to reveal to us the time of the Second Coming. During His incarnation, even Jesus did not know the time set for His return: "But of that day and hour no one knows, not even the angels of heaven, nor the Son, but the Father alone" (Matt. 24:36). He reminded the disciples just prior to His ascension that it was not God's will for them to know when He will come back to establish His kingdom: "It is not for you to know times or epochs which the Father has fixed by His own authority" (Acts 1:7).

It is best we don't know the precise time of Jesus' return; otherwise our motivation might be compromised. We could either become complacent, knowing it might be centuries before His return, or panicky, knowing He's coming back tomorrow. But living with a scriptural sense of imminence eliminates both extremes and allows us to live and minister with an attitude of expectancy.

How Should Christ's Imminent Return Affect Our Living?

The truth of our Lord's imminent coming should motivate us to be godly, watchful pursuers of righteousness. Such a desire to please Him is the mark of every genuine believer. One important incentive to obey Him is the realization that someday we will stand before His judgment seat and give an account for what we've done: "Therefore also we have as our ambition, whether at home or absent, to be pleasing to Him. For we must all appear before the judgment seat of Christ, that each one may be recompensed for his deeds in the body, according to what he has done, whether good or bad" (2 Cor. 5:9-10). Our sins won't be judged at that time—that judgment already occurred at the cross. However, Christ will assess the effectiveness, dedication, devotion, and usefulness of our service (including evangelism) for Him. Therefore, we should want to meet the Lord with joyful assurance (1 John 2:28), knowing that a divine reward awaits those who look forward to His second coming (2 Tim. 4:8; cf. Phil. 3:14; 1 John 3:2-3).

A second incentive is that our Lord Himself warned His followers to be ready. You don't know the moment of His appearance, and therefore it is prudent for you to "be on the alert, for you do not know which day your Lord is coming. But be sure of this, that if the head of the house had known at what time of the night the thief was coming, he would have been on the alert and would not have allowed his house to be broken into. For this reason you must be ready too; for the Son of Man is coming at an hour when you do not think He will" (Matt. 24:42-44).

But Jesus did balance that sober warning with the promise that He will serve those disciples who have been watchful and ready for His return: "Blessed are those slaves whom the master will find on the alert when he comes; truly I say to you, that he will gird himself to serve, and have them recline at the table, and will come up and wait on them" (Luke 12:37). And that ought to be incentive enough for us to live righteously and tell others about Him.

PRIMARY DIMENSIONS TO CHRISTIAN LIVING

As vital as it is, the expectant hope that Jesus Christ will soon return cannot be our *only* motivation for testifying of our faith. We also need to exercise the day-to-day spiritual disciplines that build strength, courage, boldness, and spiritual maturity—that which makes the Gospel believable. Prayer and the intake of Scripture by reading, studying, meditating, and memorizing enable us to obey the revealed principles in God's Word. Only then will we demonstrate the power of Christ in our lives and be prepared to apply the truth in any situation when we have opportunities to witness.

With a view toward effective witness, the apostle Peter wanted believers to understand some specific dimensions of Christian character, those that help us achieve daily excellence in our spiritual disciplines. That's why he said, "Be of sound judgment and sober spirit for the purpose of prayer" (1 Pet. 4:7).

"Be of sound judgment" is translated from two Greek words that mean "to keep safe" and "the mind." Believers must guard their minds and keep them clear and fixed on spiritual priorities. That's why Paul said, "Set your mind on the things above, not on the things that are on earth" (Col. 3:2).

Because we act according to the way we think (Prov. 23:7), it's crucial to guard our minds and focus them on God and what pleases Him. Otherwise, we easily lose our way and succumb to the various self-indulgent, deceptive, and demonic influences of the world.

Several well-known New Testament verses tell us, in effect, how we can avoid such a pitfall, protect our minds, and please the Lord (Phil. 4:8; Col. 3:16; Titus 2:11-12).

Making our minds captive to Christ (2 Cor. 10:5) and His Word (Josh. 1:8) keeps them safe and allows us to see things from God's perspective. That's how the Spirit gives us sanctified discernment and protects us from accepting doctrinal fads and errors or being foolishly indifferent toward the truth.

But Peter stresses that we need more than sound judgment—we also need to be of "sober spirit." That means we must be alert and take spiritual matters seriously. Jesus used the same term elsewhere to urge His followers to "be on the alert" (Matt. 24:42) and "keep watching" (26:41).

The combination of godly thinking and spiritual alertness is essential in any believer's life "for the purpose of prayer" (1 Pet. 4:7). We can't have a full and effective prayer life if our thinking is cluttered, confused, self-centered, or preoccupied with temporal pursuits instead of God's truth and His purposes. We will have a deep and satisfying communion with God only when we think biblically.

Continual communion with God that is informed by godly attitudes, which have been shaped by godly thinking, is therefore the foundation of a Christian's useful ministry. When you are diligent to absorb God's Word daily by reading, studying, and meditating, godly responses to all the challenges in your life will become second nature. When the three dimensions of sound judgment, spiritual alertness, and prayerful communion are present and working together in your life, you'll have an overwhelming sense of God's presence and will manifest spiritual power that will influence others for Christ and give integrity to your witness.

THE IMPACT OF REAL LOVE

A right relationship with God, as we have just described it, should result in a sincere love for other people. The apostle Peter makes that conclusion when he writes, "Above all, keep fervent in your love for one another, because love covers a multitude of sins" (1 Pet. 4:8). Here "love" mainly refers to believers' relationships with one another, but it also has an important bearing on evangelism. Jesus taught His disciples, "By this all men will know that you are My disciples, if you have love for one another" (John 13:35). Love is the substance of the Christian's witness to the world.

Paul issued similar commands: "Beyond all these things put on love, which is the perfect bond of unity" (Col. 3:14); "make my joy complete by being of the same mind, maintaining the same love, united in spirit, intent on one purpose" (Phil. 2:2).

The love Peter describes is called "fervent" and denotes the same kind of maximum effort a runner exerts in stretching and straining to win a race. Such intense love is sacrificial, not sentimental. It means believers must be prepared to love those whom it's difficult to love, even when it might sometimes be costly and seem irrational. It requires stretching all our spiritual muscles, even when those we reach out to respond with insult, injury, and misunderstanding.

The second half of 1 Peter 4:8 plainly states the reason we are to love one another: "because love covers a multitude of sins." This indicates a self-evident truth about love: by its very nature it tends to forgive all kinds of sins (cf. Prov. 10:12; Eph. 2:4). We need this reminder because as members of the Body of Christ we still sin against one another, which causes strife and division and harms our testimony to the world. Love is the only thing that can maintain or restore Christian unity because love forgives.

In the New Testament, *love* indicates volition in the spiritual and redemptive realm. God chose to love us when He saved us (John 3:16; 1 John 4:19). "God demonstrates His own love toward us, in that while we were yet sinners, Christ died for us" (Rom. 5:8). God expects those He has loved to follow His example and show their love for Him and others—not only fellow believers, but also those they seek to reach with the Gospel.

Thus the first stage of developing a proper attitude for evangelism is to understand and carry out our responsibilities as Christians in a hostile society. That means realizing we are already in the last days and that our Lord and Savior could return at any time. With that as an incentive, we are to hold ourselves and other believers accountable for holy living that overflows in God-honoring evangelism of the lost. The apostle Peter summarized again in his second letter what our task is between now and Christ's return: "Since you look for these things, be diligent to be found by Him in peace, spotless and blameless . . . grow in the grace and knowledge of our Lord and Savior Jesus Christ" (2 Pet. 3:14, 18).

Chapter 2

OUR TESTIMONY
AS SALT AND LIGHT

People's conduct, whether they are Christians or non-Christians, affects the lives of others with whom they live. Sometimes the influence is positive; at other times it is quite negative. The following two stories from Greek mythology aptly illustrate this basic principle. An invisible goddess once came to earth and left behind tangible blessings wherever she went. Charred trees she passed sprouted new leaves; flowers filled barren pathways after she walked through; stagnant pools became fresh and parched meadows green after she passed by.

Another account describes what happened when a princess was sent as a gift to a king. In appearance she was as beautiful as a goddess, and her breath smelled like fine perfume. But since infancy she had fed on nothing but poison, which permeated her being and contaminated the air around her. If she breathed on a swarm of bees, they would perish; if she picked a flower, it would wilt and die; if any bird flew too close, it would fall dead at her feet.

Obviously you and I should want our words, actions, and very presence automatically to produce positive results. In no way should believers ever want to have the kind of negative influence that accompanied the princess in the Greek myth. Even though we live, work, study, and play in this world, we are not supposed to reflect its values and attitudes (John 17:15-16, 18; 1 John 2:15). Because of who we are, we must influence the world toward salvation and God's standards of righteousness, not toward more selfishness, amorality, and materialism. We are to be in the world but not of the world.

Once we develop a biblical attitude toward our responsibilities in a spiritually hostile, morally decaying world, that attitude will inevitably help shape our approach toward evangelism. Jesus' own words in the Sermon on the Mount express for us in picturesque language the *positive* influence we will have on the world:

> *"You are the salt of the earth; but if the salt has become tasteless, how will it be made salty again? It is good for nothing any more, except to be thrown out and trampled under foot by men. You are the light of the world. A city set on a hill cannot be hidden; nor do men light a lamp, and put it under the peck-measure, but on the lampstand; and it gives light to all who are in the house. Let your light shine before men in such a way that they may see your good works, and glorify your Father who is in heaven."*
>
> —Matt. 5:13-16

THE ESSENCE OF THE BELIEVER

Most of us realize that the contemporary world, with its increasingly corrupt culture and its darker and darker outlook, needs spiritual salt and light. Preacher and commentator G. Campbell Morgan reminded believers of an earlier generation: "Jesus, looking out over the multitudes of His day, saw the corruption, the disintegration of life at every point, its breakup, its spoilation; and, because of His love of the multitudes, He knew the thing that they needed most was salt in order that the corruption should be arrested. He saw them also wrapped in gloom, sitting in darkness, groping amid mists and fogs. He knew that they needed, above everything else . . . light" (*The Gospel According to Matthew* [New York: Revell, 1929], 46). If the people of Jesus' time desperately needed salt and light, isn't it obvious that people in our day need the moral preservative and spiritual illumination that Christians, by God's help, can bring?

In Matthew 5:13-14 the Greek pronouns translated "you" are in both verses emphatic *and* plural. The emphatic form means that believers are the only persons in a culture who can truly be salt and light to it. Unless God's people are salt and light, the work of retarding moral corruption and dispelling spiritual darkness will not get done.

The plural indicates that Christ wants His entire Body, the church, to be influencing the world. Isolated grains of salt and individual beams of light have little effect. But when many grains of salt and many beams of light are joined together and dispersed throughout the world, positive and significant change is on a much wider scale.

I saw the necessity of concerted teamwork portrayed well years ago by a magazine article and its accompanying series of pictures. The article explained how a four-year-old boy had wandered from his Kansas farmhouse and into an adjacent wheat field when no one was paying attention. The first picture showed how vast the field was. The second one highlighted the boy's distressed mother sitting inside their house. His parents had searched for him all day, but he was too short to be seen in the midst of the shafts of wheat. A third photo depicted the dozens of friends and neighbors who had formed a human chain the following morning to continue the search through the wheat field. The final picture in the series showed the distraught father holding the lifeless boy who had not been found until after he had died of exposure. The caption under the fourth picture stated, "Oh God, if only we had joined hands sooner."

Many people are spiritually lost due to the sinful preoccupations of this world, and they can't find their way to the Father's house unless believers sweep through the world, searching collectively to rescue them.

When Jesus said, "You are the salt of the earth. . . . You are the light of the world" (Matt. 5:13-14), He was simply stating a fact. The elements of salt and light symbolize what believers *are*. The only issue open to question is whether or not Christ's own will act faithfully as *pungent* salt and *penetrating* light in a dying world.

Jesus is "the true light which, coming into the world, enlightens every man" (John 1:9). And He later told the disciples, "While I am in the world, I am the light of the world" (John 9:5). However, now that Christ has left the earth, it is the responsibility of believers to shine forth His reflected light: "You were formerly darkness, but now you are light in the Lord; walk as children of light" (Eph. 5:8; cf. Col. 1:13).

By definition, an influence is different from whatever it seeks to affect, which means that if we live as salt and light, we will be different from the world upon which we are called to have an impact. We cannot be the salt that retards moral corruption and spiritual decline if we are not holy. We cannot be the light that brings truth to dark places if we fail to honor the truth of God.

The Responsibility of Being Salt

In a variety of ways Jesus' first-century listeners would have understood His expression "salt of the earth" (Matt. 5:13) to refer to a valuable commodity. Roman soldiers were paid in salt, from which practice the saying "not worth his salt" originated. In many ancient societies, sharing salt at a meal symbolized a mutual responsibility of friendship and concern. Because of its preservative nature, the mineral was often used in Bible times symbolically to authenticate a covenant, similar to the contemporary practice of notarizing contracts (cf. Lev. 2:13; 2 Chron. 13:5). Therefore Christ's audience would have understood, though incompletely, that believers were to have a crucial function in the world because salt represented a valuable commodity.

What specific trait of salt did Jesus most intend to associate with spiritual character? Commentators through the centuries have made a number of suggestions. Some have said He was connecting its white color with personal purity (Christians should be pure). Some have said He was associating salt's taste with the sort of divine flavor believers should add to the world (they should add an attractiveness to the Gospel). Others have said Jesus was referring to the sting salt gives to a wound (believers should be faithful to the Word, even when doing so offends the unbeliever). Still others have said Jesus was primarily pointing to the thirst salt creates (Christians' lives ought to produce a thirst for God in the lives of unbelievers). All of the preceding observations have some validity, but they still fall short of the Lord's main emphasis.

The primary comparison Christ was making between salt and the

Christian's life is that just as salt is a preservative, the believer is a preserving influence in the world. Christ's followers, as part of their primary responsibility to live godly lives and proclaim the Gospel, can be used to save sinners and thus by their growing influence will actually help slow the moral and spiritual decay brought on by the world's culture.

We must remember that the opportunity for Christians to be preservatives is relatively brief. When God's people are raptured out of the world, the wicked power of Satan's kingdom will be unleashed in an unprecedented manner (2 Thess. 2:7-12). After that, it will take just seven years for the world to slide to the brink of hell (see Dan. 9:27; Rev. 6—19).

In the meantime, those who know Jesus Christ can greatly influence the world for good. His agents of salt have done so at specific times in the past. Martyn Lloyd-Jones writes:

> Most competent historians are agreed in saying that what undoubtedly saved [England] from a revolution such as that experienced in France at the end of the eighteenth century was nothing but the Evangelical Revival. This was not because anything was done directly, but because masses of individuals had become Christians and were living this better life and had this higher outlook. The whole political situation was affected, and the great Acts of Parliament which were passed in the last [nineteenth] century were mostly due to the fact that there were such large numbers of individual Christians found in the land. (*Studies in the Sermon on the Mount*, Vol. 1 [Grand Rapids, Mich.: Eerdmans, 1971], 157)

A more individual example of one who was salt to everyone is the story of Helen Ewing. She was saved at a young age and completely submitted to the lordship of Jesus Christ. She was only twenty-two when God took her home to heaven, and it's said that all of her native Scotland wept for her. Helen had planned to serve God as a missionary in Europe but was unable to fulfill that dream. From a human standpoint she had no prominent talents, and she never traveled far from home. Yet during her brief years she was used by God in the lives of hundreds who received Christ, and she influenced many missionaries. Those fellow laborers mourned her passing because they realized a great channel of their spiritual strength was gone.

Helen had faithfully risen every day at 5 A.M. to study Scripture and pray. Her diary listed more than 300 missionaries whom she regularly prayed for by name. She had a positive, godly influence everywhere she went. People invariably stopped or became ashamed of their sinful speech and behavior when she was around. A friend later said that while Helen was at Glasgow University she left the fragrance of Christ wherever she went. Helen Ewing's entire life and ministry was characterized by her being the Lord's salt.

The Task of Being Light

Christ also declared to all believers, "You are the light of the world" (Matt. 5:14). The quality of spiritual light possesses some definite contrasts to spiritual salt. Light depicts divine truth being directly communicated whereas salt is an indirect influence. Light works mostly through the proclamation of truth, while salt works indirectly through how we live. Light generally has a more positive ministry than salt does. Light uncovers what is sinful and false, *and* it points toward what is righteous and true. In contrast, salt is primarily negative, able to slow corruption but unable to change it into incorruption. Hence believers again need to realize that they are light *as well as* salt to those now outside of Christ.

God gives Christians His light not simply so they may have it, but so they may live by it. The psalmist affirms, "Thy word is a lamp to my feet, and a light to my path" (Ps. 119:105). And the apostle John encourages and admonishes us with these words: "God is light, and in Him there is no darkness at all. If we say that we have fellowship with Him and yet walk in the darkness, we lie and do not practice the truth; but if we walk in the light as He Himself is in the light, we have fellowship with one another, and the blood of Jesus His Son cleanses us from all sin" (1 John 1:5-7). God's light to us is both His fully inspired, written revelation—the Bible—and His Son Jesus Christ, the ever-living Light of the world (see John 1:5, 9).

We who know God are to proclaim His light to a sin-darkened world, just as Christ came "to shine upon those who sit in darkness and the shadow of death" (Luke 1:79). Those who genuinely receive that light are to reflect it to others, as expressed in this paraphrase of 2 Corinthians 4:6: "God, who first ordered the light to shine in the darkness, has flooded our hearts with His light. We now can enlighten men only because we can give them knowledge of the glory of God as we have seen it in the face of Jesus Christ." Christians will influence others with the light of divine truth if they stand out from the darkness and prove themselves "to be blameless and innocent, children of God above reproach in the midst of a crooked and perverse generation, among whom you appear as lights in the world" (Phil. 2:15).

Because God has freely offered the Gospel to all people, He did not send His Son to be a secret or hidden treasure. Instead, Christ came so that all would have opportunity to receive His light (cf. John 1:9). Many will, in unbelief, reject the light and those who deliver it, but it is still our task to shine as lights.

In Matthew 5:14 Jesus in effect describes believers who are shining as lights: "A city set on a hill cannot be hidden." Everyone in the region can see such a city. On any typical day its buildings are visible in the daylight, and its lights shine out brightly during the night. That makes the city's presence almost impossible to miss, which should also be true for God's people. A secret Christian is as incongruous as a hidden light. Believers as lights are to be displayed and shining forth, not covered.

CHALLENGES TO BEING SALT AND LIGHT

If you're a believer, you cannot lose your salvation (John 10:27-28), just as salt and light can't lose their essential properties. But you can become ineffective for the Lord when you allow the distractions of sin to pollute your life. Jesus illustrated this truth by noting in

Matthew 5:13 that salt can become tasteless if contaminated by other minerals. Although Christians in Matthew 5 are identified as salt and elsewhere are called righteous and godly (e.g., Rom. 4:4-8; 2 Cor. 5:17; Eph. 1:3-14; 2 Pet. 1:3-4), they sometimes fail to be what they are (cf. Rom. 7:15-25).

With our great responsibilities to be salt to the world, there are always challenges to fulfilling that testimony. If we succumb frequently to temptations toward impurity, we can't expect to be pure influences on the world. We can't bring God's Word to bear on people's lives if we ourselves let the busyness of life crowd out time to read, study, and meditate on Scripture. In the long run our challenge is to prayerfully ask God to help us remain His faithful disciples who make a difference for the Gospel. Our alternative is to lose our saltiness and effectiveness and become disqualified for service (cf. 1 Cor. 9:27).

Like salt, light cannot lose its essence, but it too is constantly at risk of becoming obscured in the believer's life. That's why Jesus instructed that His followers must not "light a lamp, and put it under the peck-measure, but on the lampstand; and it gives light to all who are in the house" (Matt. 5:15). A lamp that is placed under a basket cannot be useful for reading and is basically useless for any other purpose.

No matter what the reason, if we fail to live as spiritual lights, we exhibit unfaithfulness to Christ. Our desire should continually be to walk with Him and thereby defeat all challenges against living as salt and light in the world. When that is true of us, we won't be tasteless, ineffective, or useless servants in God's kingdom.

GLORIFYING GOD AS HIS LIGHTS

Whenever you let your light shine before others, whether it's by presenting the truth to them or by living the truth before them, it is something God does through you. When your family, friends, and neighbors see that kind of testimony from you, they will see Jesus' command in Matthew 5:16 fulfilled: "Let your light shine before men in such a way that they may see your good works, and glorify your Father who is in heaven."

Jesus' final phrase in verse 16 states the real purpose for your being light (and salt) in the world—so other men and women will glorify God. Your good words and deeds are not to bring praise and attention to yourself but to magnify God's grace and power. Your testimony should cause others to glorify God and—if the Spirit draws them—turn to Him in repentance and saving faith. That is the ultimate way they will give praise to the Lord as the source of their salvation.

When we live as salt and light before the world, the more frequent response from unbelievers is to react with skepticism or indifference, at times even with hostile opposition. The apostle Paul experienced positive and negative reactions to his ministry of evangelism. But his testimony was undeterred because he knew that he and other believers would manifest "the sweet aroma of the knowledge of [Christ] in every place. For we are a fragrance of Christ to God among those who are being saved and among those who are perishing; to the one an aroma from death to death, to the other an aroma from life to life" (2 Cor. 2:14-16).

The principles and commands taught by God's Word are not to be obeyed in isolation or among other Christians only, but wherever we go. We "are a chosen race, a royal priesthood, a holy nation, a people for God's own possession, that [we] may proclaim the excellencies of Him who has called [us] out of darkness into His marvelous light" (1 Pet. 2:9). God has chosen us to be His agents to proclaim the Gospel to the world. The unsaved have no other way of knowing Christ except through the testimony of what believers are—the salt of the earth and the light of the world.

Chapter 3

PRAYING FOR THE LOST

Pleading for the salvation of people who do not know Christ is very high on God's priority list of what believers should be praying for. Evangelistic prayer is both a spiritual duty and a commitment that requires much time and energy. C. H. Spurgeon wrote of its difficulty and admonished us not to neglect it:

> One more thing, *the soul-winner must be a master of the art of prayer*. You cannot bring souls to God if you go not to God yourself. You must get your battle-axe, and your weapons of war, from the armoury of sacred communication with Christ. If you are much alone with Jesus, you will catch His Spirit; you will be fired with the flame that burned in His breast, and consumed His life. You will weep with the tears that fell upon Jerusalem when He saw it perishing; and if you cannot speak so eloquently as He did, yet shall there be about what you say somewhat of the same power which in Him thrilled the hearts and awoke the consciences of men. My dear hearers, especially you members of the church, I am always so anxious lest any of you should begin to lie upon your oars, and take things easy in the matters of God's kingdom. There are some of you—I bless you, and I bless God at the remembrance of you—who are in season, and out of season, in earnest for winning souls, and you are the truly wise; but I fear there are others whose hands are slack, who are satisfied to let me preach, but do not themselves preach; who take these seats, and occupy these pews, and hope the cause goes well, but that is all they do. (*The Soul Winner* [Grand Rapids, Mich.: Eerdmans, 1989 reprint], 246-247; emphasis in original)

The Old Testament contains several examples of godly men who prayed for those who were far from the Lord. Moses prayed, "Pardon, I pray, the iniquity of this people [Israel] according to the greatness of Thy lovingkindness, just as Thou also hast forgiven this people, from Egypt even until now" (Num. 14:19).

The prophet and judge Samuel also intervened in this way. "Then Samuel spoke to all the house of Israel, saying, 'If you return to the LORD with all your heart, remove the foreign gods and the Ashtaroth from among you and direct your hearts to the LORD and serve Him alone; and He will deliver you from the hand of the Philistines.' So the sons of Israel removed the Baals and the Ashtaroth and served the LORD alone. Then Samuel said, 'Gather all Israel to Mizpah, and I will pray to the LORD for you'" (1 Sam. 7:3-5; cf. 12:23).

In the New Testament, Stephen, while being stoned to death, in effect prayed for his executioners' salvation: "They went on stoning Stephen as he called upon the Lord and said, 'Lord Jesus, receive my spirit!' Then falling on his knees, he cried out with a loud voice, 'Lord, do not hold this sin against them!' And having said this, he fell asleep" (Acts 7:59-60).

The apostle Paul earnestly desired that his fellow Jews would come to know Jesus Christ: "I am telling the truth in Christ, I am not lying, my conscience testifies with me in the Holy Spirit, that I have great sorrow and unceasing grief in my heart. For I could wish that I myself were accursed, separated from Christ for the sake of my brethren, my kinsmen according to the flesh, who are Israelites" (Rom. 9:1-4). Such a profound concern inevitably expressed itself in Paul's prayer life: "Brethren, my heart's desire and my prayer to God for them is for their salvation" (Rom. 10:1).

Evangelistic praying is definitely scriptural, appropriate, and commanded for all Christians. The imperative for such praying is expounded well in 1 Timothy 2:1-8:

> First of all, then, I urge that entreaties and prayers, petitions and thanksgivings, be made on behalf of all men, for kings and all who are in authority, so that we may lead a tranquil and quiet life in

all godliness and dignity. This is good and acceptable in the sight
of God our Savior, who desires all men to be saved and to come to
the knowledge of the truth. For there is one God, and one medi-
ator also between God and men, the man Christ Jesus, who gave
Himself as a ransom for all, the testimony borne at the proper time.
And for this I was appointed a preacher and an apostle (I am
telling the truth, I am not lying) as a teacher of the Gentiles in faith
and truth. Therefore I want the men in every place to pray, lifting
up holy hands, without wrath and dissension.

Paul urges evangelistic praying by the Ephesians (Timothy was
in Ephesus when Paul wrote to him), apparently because that had
slipped way down on their priority list. The apostle had left Timothy
there to deal with this and other church problems. Right away he
needed to address the anti-evangelistic exclusivism that had made
inroads into the Ephesian assembly due to false teaching by the
Judaizers and the Gnostics (see my *1 Timothy*, MacArthur New
Testament Commentary [Chicago: Moody Press, 1995], 60-61).

Paul's words to Timothy emphasize that our main purpose on
earth is to proclaim the Gospel to *all* the lost. That is why the topic
of evangelistic praying is so important. Both the Ephesians in Paul's
day and the church today need to understand the breadth of the
Gospel's call and avoid any form of exclusivism that would hinder
evangelism. We can attain such a balanced perspective if we begin by
knowing and applying five elements that Paul sees as necessary in
praying for the lost.

PRAYING FOR THE LOST: WHAT IS IT?

The apostle Paul defines the essence of praying for the unsaved by
listing four terms: "entreaties and prayers, petitions and thanksgivings" (1 Tim. 2:1). "Entreaties" is from the Greek root word that
means "to lack" or "to be without something." When we realize
something is missing, such as a saving relationship with Jesus Christ
in the lives of so many people, we should pray that God would pro-

vide the missing element—in that case, saving faith. The critical need to reach such a vast number with the Gospel ought especially to make us plead with God to complete the task.

"Prayers" is used in Scripture only in reference to God and thus denotes the unique aspect of worship and reverence. Evangelistic praying directs worship toward Him because when God answers it and saves sinners, all immediately glorify Him (cf. 2 Cor. 4:15).

"Petitions" is the noun form of a Greek verb that elsewhere (Rom. 8:26; Heb. 7:25) speaks of Christ's and the Holy Spirit's intercession for believers by identifying with and participating in their needs and struggles. Thus authentic evangelistic praying will not be detached and impersonal but will contain empathy and compassion for those for whom the petitions are offered. As we intercede on behalf of unsaved family, friends, and coworkers, we will sincerely seek to understand the seriousness of their lost condition and the magnitude of whatever pain and hopelessness they might be experiencing.

Finally, "thanksgivings" require that our evangelistic praying be characterized by gratitude that God has offered the gospel message, that He has chosen us to be His evangelists, and that His Spirit draws some to faith and repentance.

If any of those enriching facets are missing from your praying for the lost, you need to ask yourself some heart-searching questions. Do you understand the extent of the unsaved person's desperate condition, what he or she is missing? Do you really want to see God glorified by saving sinners? Are you thankful for the opportunity and privilege God has given you of sharing the Gospel with those inside your circle of influence? You may have been unaware of or indifferent to such promptings in the past, but now you need to ask the Lord's help in being more sensitive to those concerns as you pray.

PRAYING FOR THE LOST: WHAT IS THE SCOPE OF IT?

We should never arbitrarily place limits to our evangelistic praying. If Paul told Timothy that prayer is to "be made on behalf of all men, for kings and all who are in authority" (1 Tim. 2:1b-2a), then it is not right for us to selfishly limit the extent of the gospel call or to restrict our evangelistic prayers. For one thing, we don't know who the elect are until after they respond to the Gospel. And Paul tells us later in this passage that God desires everyone to be saved (2:4). Elsewhere Scripture is clear that prayer for *all* who are lost is completely consistent with God's heart. Ezekiel 33:11 says He is not pleased when people die without repenting, but He is happy when they do turn to Him. In Acts 17:30 Paul told the Athenians that "God is now declaring to men that all people everywhere should repent" (cf. 3:26). Therefore, we as believers do have a responsibility to pray that the unregenerate will obey the Lord's command and accept His universal offer of salvation (Titus 2:11), and leave God's elective purpose to Him.

One group of people, however, is often easy to neglect or ignore in our evangelistic prayers—men and women in the world who serve as governmental and political leaders. Therefore Paul particularly mentions them, as if to tell Timothy and us that such people must not be excluded from our concern. We must overcome the tendency to be indifferent or even bitter toward them, which is easy to do because secular leaders are so inaccessible, often unrighteous toward their constituents, and wicked and frequently contemptuous toward God and His Word. For example, when President Bill Clinton personally establishes the month of June as Gay and Lesbian Pride month, he is in open defiance of the honor and the command of God. And even believers begin to view him as the enemy rather than the mission field.

But such a tendency is sinful because of the special authority and responsibility leaders have. We should certainly ask God to grant them wisdom and discernment in their official decisions and actions. However, we should apply Paul's words in 1 Timothy 2:2 beyond simply praying that governmental leaders would be wise and just. We also need to pray that the great majority of them will repent and believe the Gospel, and honor God's Word.

The Bible is not making exceptions of evil leaders, or ones we disagree with politically. Instead, the epistles instruct Christians to be loyal and submissive to their governments (Rom. 13:1-5; 1 Pet. 2:17). If more believers in recent decades had devoted as much of their efforts to evangelistic prayer "for kings and all who are in authority" as they did toward partisan strategizing (attempting to win the so-called culture wars through political activism), we might have seen a genuine, measurable improvement in government and society (cf. 2 Cor. 10:4). If nations are to experience positive changes in morality and spirituality, sinners must be saved, and that calls for faithful prayer.

PRAYING FOR THE LOST: WHAT IS THE BENEFIT?

The apostle Paul provides incentive for his command that believers pray for all who are lost, even those in positions of authority: "so that we may lead a tranquil and quiet life in all godliness and dignity" (1 Tim. 2:2b). Essentially, when the church is fully obedient in praying for the lost, the benefit will be societal conditions favorable for its outreach efforts.

When you pray for your leaders, you're likely not thinking of ways to disobey or overthrow their legal authority. Instead, you are becoming the kinds of peacemakers who please the Lord Jesus and match Paul's instructions to Titus: "Remind them to be subject to rulers, to authorities, to be obedient, to be ready for every good deed, to malign no one, to be uncontentious, gentle, showing every consideration for all men. For we also once were foolish ourselves, disobedient, deceived, enslaved to various lusts and pleasures, spending our life in malice and envy, hateful, hating one another" (Titus 3:1-3).

The second benefit that comes to God's people when they pray for *everyone* who is lost is that the world begins to see the church as having the positive traits set forth in Titus 3:1-2. People in society will see Christians as friends who seek their welfare, not their harm. As the lost turn in increasing numbers to faith in Christ, in answer to believers' heartfelt prayers, that opens the possibility for additional fruit in evangelism and generally more favorable conditions for the church's ministry.

Such an atmosphere for the church in society, as it prays diligently, consistently, and compassionately for the salvation of all,
decreases the potential for hostility and contributes to our being free
to minister without external and internal disturbances ("a tranquil
and quiet life," 1 Tim. 2:2b). Proclaiming the Gospel and all of God's
truth uncompromisingly does not mean we have to disrupt national
life or be jailed as civil agitators. If we are persecuted as believers, it
should be only be because we are faithful in obeying Jesus Christ (cf.
1 Pet. 2:13-23).

If the church is being obedient to Christ and enjoying a favorable atmosphere in which to evangelize, that situation will be further
enhanced by its members living in "godliness and dignity" (1 Tim.
2:2b). "Godliness" here refers to the attitude of reverence toward
God, and "dignity" means living with a strong sense of moral earnest-
ness. Holy motives will lead to righteous behavior, and that will result
in Christians' having an effective testimony before the world.

The apostle Paul also urged the Thessalonian believers to be
faithful in living quiet and respectable lives: "make it your ambition
to lead a quiet life and attend to your own business and work with
your hands" (1 Thess. 4:11; cf. 2 Thess. 3:11-12). The unsaved
around us should view us as peace lovers who conscientiously fulfill
our duties and demonstrate loving concern for their welfare, both
physical and spiritual. We may rightly hate the evil world system, but
we should pray for the salvation of all who are enslaved in it.

PRAYING FOR THE LOST: WHY?

Paul continues in his instructions to Timothy regarding evangelistic
prayer by presenting one of Scripture's most definitive statements on
God's saving purpose. It contains five reasons that Christians must
pray for the lost:

> *This is good and acceptable in the sight of God our Savior, who*
> *desires all men to be saved and to come to the knowledge of the*
> *truth. For there is one God, and one mediator also between God*

*and men, the man Christ Jesus, who gave Himself as a ransom
for all, the testimony given at the proper time. And for this I was
appointed a preacher and an apostle (I am telling the truth, I am
not lying) as a teacher of the Gentiles in faith and truth.*

—1 Tim. 2:3-7

Praying for the Lost Is Morally Right

God in good faith issues a general call to all sinners and genuinely
desires them to embrace salvation: "'As I live!' declares the Lord God,
'I take no pleasure in the death of the wicked, but rather that the
wicked turn from his way and live. Turn back, turn back from your
evil ways! Why then will you die, O house of Israel?'" (Ezek. 33:11).
God sees evangelistic praying as a noble and spiritually right
endeavor. ("Good" in 1 Timothy 2:3 speaks of what is intrinsically
and morally good.) And if we as believers are honest, our consciences
will agree, and we will want to share God's desire that all sinners be
saved (cf. Rom. 9:3; 10:1). Unbelievers live prideful or futile lives
and, unless they're converted, will suffer in eternal agony, forever
separated from the Lord after they die. Given the truth of that, we
ought to be praying consistently and earnestly for them.

Praying for the Lost Is Consistent with God's Desire

If we have a biblical understanding of God's sovereignty in election
and accept the truth that "He chose us in Him before the foundation
of the world.... In love he predestined us to adoption as sons" (Eph.
1:4-5), then we realize that His desire for the salvation of all is somehow different from His eternal purpose that not everyone actually
will be saved.

A similar kind of distinction between desire and purpose exists
at the human level. This distinction is illustrated to a limited extent
quite regularly in our daily lives. There are undoubtedly many work-
days in which we would rather take the day off. But our sense of
responsibility and higher purpose compels us to report to work anyway. In a parallel fashion, God's eternal purpose in His plan of
redemption transcends His desire. (Of course, unlike human beings,

God is never compelled by circumstances beyond His control to choose what He does not desire. For Him, everything is in accord with His sovereign purpose.)

God sincerely wishes that all men and women would turn to Him in saving faith; yet He chose only the elect "out of the world" (John 17:6) and passed over other sinners, leaving them in their depravity and wickedness (cf. Rom. 1:18-32). As a result, they are damned solely because of their sin and rejection of God. He is in no way to blame for such unbelief and is not happy that many people ultimately choose hell. However, God will receive glory even when unbelievers are damned (cf. Rom. 9:22-23).

How this great program of redemption and condemnation, with its apparent paradoxes and divine mysteries, unfolds in a way that is completely consistent with God's will can be answered only by Him. Believers who seek to be faithful witnesses as they embrace God's truth must do so by faith in His Word, trusting in such profound declarations as this:

> *Oh, the depth of the riches both of the wisdom and knowledge of God! How unsearchable are His judgments and unfathomable His ways! For who has known the mind of the Lord, or who became His counselor? Or who has first given to Him that it might be paid back to him again? For from Him and through Him and to Him are all things. To Him be the glory forever. Amen.*
> —Rom. 11:33-36

Since the Lord "desires all men to be saved" (1 Tim. 2:4; cf. Matt. 23:37), it is not our concern to know if someone is elect before praying for that person's salvation. We may pray for anyone who is unsaved, knowing that such prayers are fully consistent with God's desire. After all, "The LORD is gracious and merciful; slow to anger and great in lovingkindness. The LORD is good to all, and His mercies are over all His works" (Ps. 145:8-9).

Praying for the Lost Reflects God's Uniqueness

We are told in this era of inclusivism and religious and philosophical pluralism that Judaism, Islam, Buddhism, Hinduism, and countless other major and minor religions are equally valid and ultimately provide a path to heaven and God. If that's true, then Christians really don't need to evangelize because the many ways of salvation will eventually "save" most people. But believers know Scripture teaches there is only one true God and Savior (see Deut. 4:35, 39; 6:4; Isa. 43:10; 44:6; 45:5-6, 21-22; 46:9; 1 Cor. 8:4, 6). Thus there is a need for interceding and asking that people recognize and accept Him as the only source of salvation (cf. Acts 4:12).

Praying for the Lost Is Consistent with the Person of Christ

Only through "the man Christ Jesus" (1 Tim. 2:5) can people truly draw near to God. As the perfect God-man (the Greek construction indicates the translation, "Christ Jesus, Himself man"), Christ brings God and man together. The book of Hebrews calls Him the mediator of a new and better covenant (Heb. 8:6; 9:15; 12:24). People cannot approach God through any other mediator—angels, saints, Mary—and they cannot achieve salvation by any other means—good works, legalistic or ritualistic religious practices, transcendental meditation—but only by placing their faith in Christ's atoning work (John 3:16; Acts 10:43; Rom. 3:21-26; 5:1; 1 Pet. 1:18-21). Therefore it is entirely appropriate and necessary for us to ask God that sinners' hearts embrace Jesus' declaration, "I am the way, and the truth, and the life; no one comes to the Father, but through Me" (John 14:6).

Praying for the Lost Reflects the Fullness of the Atonement

The nature of our Lord's atonement, when scripturally understood, ought to be another motivation for us to pray more fervently and confidently for the unsaved. All people, without their realizing it, are benefited by the all-sufficient character of Christ's atoning work (cf. Matt. 5:45; Acts 14:17). His substitutionary death, in which He was sacrificed in our place to bear our sin in order to satisfy God's justice, is sufficient for all mankind. In the words of the apostle Paul, He "gave Himself as a ransom for all" (1 Tim. 2:6). However, as we have already implied from our discussion of God's desire and purpose in salvation, by design the atonement is efficacious only for those who believe (cf. Matt. 22:14).

But knowing the design of Christ's atonement should in no way keep us from praying that the Gospel would be preached to everyone without distinction (Mark 16:15), that the divine offer of the water of life would be freely made to all (Rev. 22:17), and that trust in Jesus as Savior and Lord would be encouraged for every person (1 Tim. 4:10; 1 John 4:14).

Christ's work on the cross accomplished everything God in eternity past decided it would concerning the salvation of sinners. Unbelievers who reject the Gospel do not at all thwart God's purposes in His sovereign plan of redemption. The prophet Isaiah records, "I am God, and there is no one like Me, declaring the end from the beginning and from ancient times things which have not been done, saying, 'My purpose will be established, and I will accomplish all My good pleasure'" (Isa. 46:9b-10). Therefore, we can pray with confidence that God will save all those He has chosen for redemption from before the world began (cf. John 17:12; Acts 13:48).

PRAYING FOR THE LOST: WHAT SHOULD BE OUR ATTITUDE?

Paul concludes his instructions to Timothy on the importance of praying for the lost by stressing that believers also must have the right attitude while praying: "Therefore I want the men in every place to pray, lifting up holy hands, without wrath and dissension" (1 Tim. 2:8).

First the apostle commands male leaders of the church to lead in prayers for the lost whenever such petitions are offered. His phrase "in every place" refers to the official worship assembly of the church, as it does the three other times it's used in Paul's letters (see 1 Cor. 1:2; 2 Cor. 2:14; 1 Thess. 1:8).

Second, Paul emphasizes that evangelistic praying must flow

from a holy life. Although Old Testament believers often prayed with raised hands (e.g., 1 Kings 8:22; Neh. 8:6; Ps. 134:2; Isa. 1:15), the reference here to "holy hands" means sanctified activities of life, not just a prayer posture. Such a lifestyle is the prerequisite for effective prayer of any kind (cf. Ps. 66:18). Of course, holy living excludes any attitudes that would stir up "wrath and dissension" and ruin proper praying for the lost.

History is filled with role models of those who prayed for the lost. The greatest model was the Lord Jesus Himself, who "interceded for the transgressors" (Isa. 53:12) and who prayed, "Father, forgive them; for they do not know what they are doing" (Luke 23:34).

In more recent centuries other models of evangelistic prayer warriors worth emulating have been the Scottish Reformer John Knox ("Give me Scotland or I die!"), the English evangelist George Whitefield ("O Lord, give me souls or take my soul!"), and the missionary to India Henry Martyn ("I cannot endure existence if Jesus is to be so dishonored").

God honors our prayers for the lost. The Holy Spirit drew 3,000 souls to Him on the Day of Pentecost and has regenerated thousands of others throughout church history. A notable example was Saul of Tarsus, who stood by and gave his consent to Stephen's fatal stoning. We can easily surmise that Saul, who became Paul the apostle, was eventually saved in answer to Stephen's dying prayer, "Lord, do not hold this sin against them!" (Acts 7:60). Authentic and thorough evangelism has to start with our praying for the lost.

PART TWO

WHAT WE

PROCLAIM

AND

DEFEND

Chapter 4

WHO IS GOD?

In a cogent, perceptive analysis of contemporary evangelistic practice, Baptist pastor Walter Chantry wrote these words a generation ago:

> Much of modern preaching is anaemic, with the life-blood of God's nature absent from the message. Evangelists centre their message upon man. Man has sinned and missed a great blessing. If man wants to retrieve his immense loss he must act thus and so. But the Gospel of Christ is very different. It begins with God and His glory. It tells men that they have offended a holy God, who will by no means pass by sin. It reminds sinners that the only hope of salvation is to be found in the grace and power of this same God. Christ's Gospel sends men to beg pardon of the Holy One. (*Today's Gospel: Authentic or Synthetic?* [Edinburgh: Banner of Truth, 1970], 25)

The essence of the faith we proclaim and defend must begin with God, but who is God? For Sigmund Freud, the father of contemporary psychoanalysis, God was simply an invention of the human mind in response to three basic fears—the fear of nature, the fear of relationships, and the fear of death. According to his theory, people have continually looked for refuge in a God who would solve their troubles and protect them. It is that strong desire that caused people to invent the God of the Bible. But that is contrary to what Scripture says about man's nature. Humanity has consistently sought to escape accountability to God's standards (cf. Gen. 3:8). Men and women would prefer that the biblical God *not* exist, even though there is an essential knowledge of Him placed within each person, as Romans 1:19-20 says: "that which is known about God is evident within them;

for God made it evident to them. For since the creation of the world His invisible attributes, His eternal power and divine nature, have been clearly seen, being understood through what has been made, so that they are without excuse." Instead, people persist in rejecting God's self-revelation because they do "not see fit to acknowledge God" (Rom. 1:28).

THE ONE TRUE GOD

In spite of erroneous theories and speculations by Freud and other secular thinkers, believers know that the unsaved must accept the existence of God by faith: "He who comes to God must believe that He is" (Heb. 11:6). But that is just a first step toward saving faith. Genuine belief in God will go beyond the first step of realizing there is a God and will acknowledge the only true God, revealed in the Bible.

Embracing the true God by faith means sinners must begin to learn what the Lord taught Job:

> *Where were you when I laid the*
> *foundation of the earth?*
> *Tell Me, if you have understanding,*
> *Who set its measurements,*
> *since you know?*
> *Or who stretched the line on it?*
> *On what were its bases sunk?*
> *Or who laid its cornerstone,*
> *When the morning stars sang together*
> *And all the sons of God shouted for joy?*
> *—Job 38:4-7*

It means believing what God says to be true, based on His Word.

Our task is not to turn people to scientific evidence to prove the existence of God. There are plenty of scientific and rational evidences that make faith in God and the Bible reasonable, but such evidences have their limits. Paul Little, who was a leading teacher of evangelism and apologetics in the late 1960s and early 1970s, noted this:

It can be said with equal emphasis that you can't "prove" Napoleon by the scientific method. The reason lies in the nature of history itself and in the limitations of the scientific method. In order for something to be "proved" by the scientific method, it must be repeatable. One cannot announce a new finding to the world on the basis of a single experiment.

But history in its very nature is nonrepeatable. No man can "rerun" the beginning of the universe or bring Napoleon back or repeat the assassination of Lincoln or the crucifixion of Jesus Christ. But the fact that these events can't be "proved" by repetition does not disprove their reality as events. (*Know Why You Believe* [Downers Grove, Ill.: InterVarsity Press, 1968], 8)

When we remove all the discussion and debate about man's relationship to God, how he can know Him, and what he must do, it comes down to a person's saying, "I believe." The basis for such faith is not scientific proof but inspired Scripture. We must turn to God's Word to understand what it affirms about God's nature—that He is a Person yet a spirit, and that He is one yet manifested in three Persons.

GOD IS PERSONAL

Sinners can know God because He is knowable, as He said to the prophet Jeremiah: "You will seek Me and find Me, when you search for Me with all your heart" (Jer. 29:13). The Lord would not have said that about Himself if it were not true.

The Bible is replete with personal titles that describe God, such as Father, Shepherd, Friend, and Counselor. The original text also contains many uses of the personal pronouns He, Him, and

His to refer to God. Such usages indicate God is personal and therefore knowable. He is a spirit, but He has all the characteristics of personality—He thinks, feels, acts, relates to persons, and speaks to His creatures through Scripture. God wants to communicate with man.

GOD IS SPIRITUAL

Another crucial truth believers must proclaim about God is that He is spirit. Christ announced, "God is spirit; and those who worship Him must worship in spirit . . ." (John 4:24). Theologian Charles Hodge explains this truth as follows:

> It is impossible . . . to overestimate the importance of the truth contained in the simple proposition, God is a Spirit. It is involved in that proposition that God is immaterial. None of the properties of matter can be predicated of Him. He is not extended or divisible, or compounded, or visible, or tangible. He has neither bulk nor form. . . . In revealing, therefore, that God is a Spirit, the Bible reveals to us that no attribute of matter can be predicated of the divine essence. (*Systematic Theology*, abridged ed. [Grand Rapids, Mich.: Baker, 1988 reprint], 138-139)

To accommodate human understanding, Scripture sometimes describes God in human terms (anthropomorphisms; e.g., Ps. 89:13; Isa. 50:2; Zech. 4:10). And He revealed Himself in tangible, material forms at momentous times in redemptive history. At certain times in the Old Testament, He appeared as the *Shekinah*—the glorious, divine light in the fire and cloud. In the Gospels He appeared in the incarnate form of Jesus Christ (John 1:14, 18). However, none of those revelations portrayed the fullness of God's essence, nor did they contradict the truth that He is first and foremost invisible and spiritual (cf. 1 Tim. 1:17).

GOD IS ONE

Moses clearly announced to Israel the truth that there is only one true God: "Hear, O Israel! The LORD is our God, the LORD is one!" (Deut. 6:4; cf. Isa. 44:6). Moses knew it was crucial to the Israelites' testimony to the pagan, polytheistic nations around them that they affirm their allegiance to the only true God. Moses recalled the second commandment, in which God declared Himself to be a jealous God (Exod. 20:4-5). That meant His people were not to worship any other deity.

Jesus later echoed Moses' teaching when He told the Jewish teachers, "'Hear, O Israel; the Lord our God is one Lord; and you shall love the Lord your God with all your heart, and with all your soul, and with all your mind, and with all your strength'" (Mark 12:29-30). The Son of God wanted people to love God with undivided allegiance, and at the same time He identified Himself as God (John 10:30, 38; 12:45; 14:7-10; 17:11). (This is part of the mystery of the Trinity, which we will discuss in the next section.)

The apostle Paul underscored the importance of God's oneness:

There is no God but one. For even if there are so-called gods whether in heaven or on earth . . . yet for us there is but one God, the Father, from whom are all things, and we exist for Him; and one Lord, Jesus Christ, by whom are all things, and we exist through Him.

—1 Cor. 8:4-6

Paul also utilized the truth of God's oneness to affirm the universal offer of the Gospel: "Is God the God of Jews only? Is He not the God of Gentiles also? Yes, of Gentiles also—if indeed God is one—and He will justify the circumcised by faith and the uncircumcised through faith" (Rom. 3:29-30; cf. 1 Tim. 2:5). Scripture is thus clear that there is only one true God, and He is the only source of genuine salvation for all people.

GOD IS THREE IN ONE

Another foundational truth about God that we must proclaim is that He is one Being who exists in three Persons. This of course is the doctrine of the Trinity, which has always been a mystery unparalleled in human experience and impossible to fully understand. Some teachers have used very limited earthly analogies to try to explain it. For example, they point out that an egg has a shell, a white, and a yolk but is still one object. And water can exist in three different states— liquid, solid, or gas—but it retains the same chemical formula, H_2O. In similar fashion, according to these analogies, the Godhead consists of three Persons who minister together as one God.

Such illustrations are helpful, but they fail to provide a true explanation of how God can be three Persons in one. The majestic glory of the Triune God is infinite, and we must accept by faith what the Old Testament and particularly the New Testament teach concerning His trinity.

The Trinity in the Old Testament

The very first verse of the Bible indicates that the Godhead is plural. The English translation of Genesis 1:1 does not reflect it, but the Hebrew term (*Elohim*) rendered "God" contains a plural suffix that presents a singular God expressed as a plurality.

The plurality of the Godhead was instrumental in the creation of the universe (Gen. 1:1—2:3), and it was evident in the creation of man when God said, "Let *Us* make man in *Our* image, according to *Our* likeness" (1:26, emphases added). Also in Genesis, the Trinity is unquestionably referred to when God punished humanity for its sinful ambition that resulted in the Tower of Babel: "Come, let *Us* go down and there confuse their language, so that they may not understand one another's speech" (Gen. 11:7, emphasis added).

The different Persons of the Godhead are alluded to in many other Old Testament passages, with much of the focus being on the preincarnate Christ. Charles Hodge offers this additional insight:

We . . . find throughout the Old Testament constant mention made of a person to whom, though distinct from Jehovah as a person, the titles, attributes, and works of Jehovah are nevertheless ascribed. This person is called the angel of God, the angel of Jehovah, Adonai, Jehovah, and Elohim. He claims divine authority, exercises divine prerogatives, and receives divine homage. . . .

Besides this we have the express testimony of the inspired writers of the New Testament that the angel of the Lord, the manifested Jehovah who led the Israelites through the wilderness and who dwelt in the temple, was Christ; that is, the angel was the Word . . . who became flesh and fulfilled the work which it was predicted the Messiah should accomplish. (*Systematic Theology*, 177)

In some of the Old Testament passages where Christ actually speaks, He mentions the other two members of the Trinity: "Come near to Me, listen to this: From the first I have not spoken in secret, from the time it took place, I was there. And now the LORD God has sent Me, and His Spirit" (Isa. 48:16c; cf. Ps. 2:7; 45:7; 110:1).

The Trinity in the New Testament

Since the New Testament features the incarnation of the second member of the Trinity, and the sending of the third member to minister on earth, there is ample support for the doctrine of the Trinity. Throughout the New Testament the three Persons of the Godhead are mentioned in connection with important events and truths.

The Trinity was on display in the birth, death, and resurrection of the Lord Jesus. An angel from heaven announced to Mary, "The Holy Spirit will come upon you, and the power of the Most High will overshadow you; and for that reason the holy offspring shall be called the Son of God" (Luke 1:35).

The Father, Son, and Holy Spirit all participated in Jesus' baptism: "And it came about in those days that Jesus came from Nazareth in Galilee, and was baptized by John in the Jordan. And immediately coming up out of the water, He saw the heavens opening, and the Spirit like a dove descending upon Him; and a voice came out of the heavens: 'Thou art My beloved Son, in Thee I am well-pleased'" (Mark 1:9-11; cf. Matt. 3:13-17; Luke 3:21-22).

The resurrection of Christ was accomplished by the power of the Father (Rom. 6:4; Gal. 1:1; 1 Pet. 1:3), the Son (John 10:18), and the Holy Spirit (Rom. 8:11).

Christ's atonement for sinners also was carried out by the ministry of all three members of the Trinity. The Son offered Himself as a perfect sacrifice to the Father, and the Holy Spirit empowered Him to do so (cf. Heb. 9:14; 1 Pet. 1:1-2). Furthermore, the Father, Son, and Holy Spirit each fulfill a specific role in securing the salvation that the atonement provides for all who believe. The Father establishes believers in Jesus Christ (2 Cor. 1:21-22); the Son guarantees that they will be without blame when He returns for His own at the Rapture (1 Cor. 1:7-8); and the Spirit seals the believer's inheritance in heaven (Eph. 1:13).

Another unfathomable truth regarding the Trinity is, only one name but three Persons, as evidenced when Jesus said, "Go therefore and make disciples of all the nations, baptizing them in the name of the Father and the Son and the Holy Spirit" (Matt. 28:19). Jesus did not ascribe a separate name to each member of the Godhead but used "*the* name" to speak of all that God is and does as the Trinity.

Other aspects of the Trinity's work are also beyond our full understanding, such as how the Father and the Son were both responsible for sending the Spirit (see John 14:16-17; 15:26). J. I. Packer provides this perspective on the eternal mystery:

> Here we face the most dizzying and unfathomable truth of all, the truth of the Trinity. . . . What should we make of it? In itself, the divine tri-unity is a mystery, a transcendent fact which passes our understanding. . . .
>
> How the one eternal God is eternally both singular and plural, how Father, Son, and Spirit are personally distinct yet essentially one . . . is more than we can know, and any

attempt to "explain" it—to dispel the mystery by reasoning, as distinct from confessing it from Scripture—is bound to falsify it. Here, as elsewhere, our God is too big for his creatures' little minds. (*I Want to Be a Christian* [Wheaton, Ill.: Tyndale House, 1977], 29-30)

The only way to embrace the reality of the Triune God is to trust what His revealed Word says. Then we can direct others toward a Father who desires sinners to be saved, a Son whose death is sufficient to pay the penalty for sin, and a Holy Spirit who can bring them to saving faith. Once they begin to realize how big this God is, it should humble them to consider that they are accountable to Him for their sin and rebellion.

THE REVELATION OF GOD'S WRATH

Romans 1:18 states an important truth about the nature of God, often ignored in this era of man-centered teaching and evangelizing: "For the wrath of God is revealed from heaven against all ungodliness and unrighteousness of men, who suppress the truth in unrighteousness." God has been constantly revealing His wrath, from the beginning of human history.

The first time was in response to Adam and Eve after they disobediently ate fruit from the tree of the knowledge of good and evil and caused themselves, all of humanity after them, and the entire creation to fall under the curse of sin. The first man and woman thus had to be evicted from the Garden of Eden. In the centuries that followed, humanity became so debauched that God released His wrath again through the Flood (cf. Gen. 6:7). God has also demonstrated His wrath in destroying the gross sinfulness of Sodom and Gomorrah, sending plagues upon the Egyptians, and instituting the sacrificial system. The suffering and death of Jesus Christ was perhaps the ultimate demonstration of God's wrath. The Father's hatred for sin is so intense that for the sake of sinners He poured out His righteous fury on His beloved, sinless Son, who took their place.

The Nature of God's Wrath

If we are to be effective evangelists, we must make clear to unbelievers the nature of God's wrath against sin. His wrath is not dispensed in a detached way, or mechanistically as from an anonymous cosmic computer. On the contrary, Scripture reveals God's wrath to be the result of His intense personal reaction against sin.

Some Old Testament words describe God's holy response to human sin. For example, the Hebrew word *charah* means "to become heated up, to burn with fury." In that sense, God's wrath was directed against Israel because she practiced immoral pagan rites (Num. 25:3). His anger was deflected from the people only after Moses executed the leaders involved in those sinful rites.

The related word *charon* denotes a burning, fierce wrath. The Lord's anger burned against the Israelites when they flouted His commandments and worshiped a molten calf (Exod. 32:12).

Za'am further portrays the nature of God's wrath. It is used for someone who is furious: "God is angry with the wicked every day" (Ps. 7:11, KJV).

The apostle Paul taught that God will render "to those who are selfishly ambitious and do not obey the truth, but obey unrighteousness, *wrath* and *indignation*. There will be *tribulation* and *distress* for every soul of man who does evil" (Rom. 2:8-9, emphases added). The word translated "wrath" means "to rush along," "be in a hurry," or "breathe violently." Its biblical usage describes, for example, Pharaoh's desire to kill Moses, the rage of those who wanted to throw Jesus off a cliff, and the emotions associated with the riot at Ephesus. Similarly, God's wrath will burst forth like a consuming fire against all sinners who, without exception, disobey His law and reject and oppose the Gospel.

Why God's Wrath?

The primary reason God is constrained to unleash His wrath is that men and women sinfully reject His revelation of Himself (Rom. 1:18-21). It's not at all like the uncontrolled, irrational human rage that might lash out vengefully at an offending person. Instead, God carefully and discerningly aims His wrath at specific ungodliness and unrighteousness (cf. v. 18).

"Ungodliness" naturally occurs when people do not have a right relationship with God. Unbelievers' ungodliness manifests itself in their impiety toward Him. Their disobedience to His law, their lack of reverence, devotion, and worship, eventually leads them to idolatry and even to intense opposition of Him. That happens even though creation has provided everyone who has ever lived with enough spiritual light to recognize God's sustaining power and deity.

Unbelievers need to know that God is charging them with the most serious crime they could ever commit: "Even though they knew God, they did not honor Him as God" (v. 21). When people persist in refusing to recognize God's attributes and to acknowledge that He alone is worthy of their complete worship and allegiance, they are simply exhibiting the essence of fallen humanity and demonstrating that they deserve to be objects of God's holy wrath.

The Westminster Shorter Catechism's well-known statement tells us what mankind's responsibility is: "The chief end of man is to glorify God and enjoy Him forever" (cf. Ps. 148; 1 Cor. 10:31). But that is exactly where unregenerate men and women fall short and make themselves the objects of God's wrath.

GOD'S SOVEREIGN PLAN OF REDEMPTION

However, God in His sovereignty has shown mercy as well as wrath. According to His eternal plan, some would escape His wrath and become willing to worship and serve Him. Paul outlined that theme in Romans 9. He used Jacob and Esau to illustrate God's choice in salvation: "For though the twins [Jacob and Esau] were not yet born, and had not done anything good or bad, so that God's purpose according to His choice might stand, not because of works, but because of Him who calls, it was said to her: 'The older will serve the younger'" (vv. 11-12).

As Paul explained in Romans 4 concerning Abraham's justification (cf. Gen. 15:6), God alone, apart from human works or merit, grants redemption to all who believe. He has sovereignly purposed to love His own, and nothing can violate that plan or cause it to fail, because God is faithful to His Word.

Jews have not been the only recipients of God's grace and mercy through His plan of redemption, nor are all Jews saved. The apostle Paul explains it this way in Romans 9:6-8: "For they are not all Israel who are descended from Israel; nor are they all children because they are Abraham's descendants, but: 'Through Isaac your descendants will be named.' That is, it is not the children of the flesh who are children of God, but the children of the promise are regarded as descendants."

What a wonderful truth to share with unbelievers, that Abraham is the spiritual father of all who believe (cf. Rom. 4:11-12; Gal. 3:7). And those who become true spiritual sons and daughters of Abraham, because they have exercised the same faith as he did, will be forever secure in God's sovereign plan of redemption. Paul summarizes this truth in Romans 8:29-30: "For whom He foreknew, He also predestined to become conformed to the image of His Son, so that He would be the first-born among many brethren; and whom He predestined, these He also called; and whom He called, these He also justified; and whom He justified, these He also glorified."

GOD NEVER CHANGES

God's sovereignty in salvation is related to His unchanging character. We can count on Him as the reliable, consistent source of true redemption and all its subsequent blessings. God Himself attests to this truth: "For I, the LORD, do not change" (Mal. 3:6). And the apostle James said that with God "there is no variation, or shifting shadow" (James 1:17).

From a human perspective, change can be either good or bad. But neither one is conceivable with God. A. W. Pink described God's unwavering character this way: "[God] cannot change for the better, for He is already perfect; and being perfect, He cannot change for the worse. Altogether unaffected by anything outside Himself, improvement or deterioration is impossible. He is perpetually the same" (*The Attributes of God* [Grand Rapids, Mich.: Baker, 1975 reprint], 37).

In spite of that truth, however, some people are still confused by certain Scripture passages on sin, repentance, and salvation that seem to say God can change His mind. For instance, referring to the time prior to the Flood, Moses' narrative says, "The LORD was sorry that He had made man on the earth, and He was grieved in His heart. And the LORD said, 'I will blot out man whom I have created from the face of the land, from man to animals to creeping things and to birds of the sky; for I am sorry that I have made them'" (Gen. 6:6-7). But it was not God's character that changed in that situation. He originally created people for good works, but they chose to disobey and do evil. That choice brought sorrow to, or, as some translations say, "grieved" a holy God who is without sin (cf. Exod. 32:14; 1 Sam. 15:11; Jer. 26:3).

Another frequently misinterpreted passage concerns the repentance of Nineveh following Jonah's preaching. When God saw the inhabitants turn from their sin, He "relented concerning the calamity which He had declared He would bring upon them. And He did not do it" (Jonah 3:10). Again, that was a situation in which God's basic character did not change. It was not that He "repented" (as the King James Version translates it) but simply that He showed mercy (something He consistently does) to the Ninevites because they had turned from their sins.

Neither of those accounts are examples of how God is changeable. Rather, they are reminders that His character is holy and completely consistent. He always punishes sinful unbelief and rewards sincere, saving faith. Numbers 23:19 describes God's unalterable righteousness like this: "God is not a man, that He should lie, nor the son of man, that He should repent; has He said, and will He not do it? Or has He spoken, and will He not make it good?"

Everyone and everything created by God is subject to change. The book of Revelation tells of the extreme changes the heavens will eventually undergo (cf. 6:12-14; 8:12). It also describes how the earth will suffer drastic change in the end (8:7-11).

Both believers and unbelievers are subject to change. Most of the time genuine Christians will affirm their love for God and trust in Him, as when David said, "The LORD is my rock and my fortress and my deliverer; my God, my rock, in whom I take refuge" (2 Sam. 22:2-3). But there are other times when they, again like David, will be fearful and show a lack of trust (cf. 1 Sam. 27:1).

In the face of all such changes, we are still left with the truth that must be proclaimed to the lost: the personal Triune God does not change. Sinners who flee His wrath can be secure in His eternal plan of redemption, because God honors His Word and faithfully fulfills all His promises. Jesus told the disciples, "Have faith in God" (Mark 11:22). He was saying, "You can trust God. You can put your life in His hands." He also said, "All that the Father gives Me shall come to Me; and the one who comes to Me I will certainly not cast out" (John 6:37). And He extends that invitation with confidence to all sinners because He knows God's promise to the prophet Isaiah will be kept: "Surely, just as I have intended so it has happened, and just as I have planned so it will stand" (Isa. 14:24).

Chapter 5

THE RELIABILITY OF SCRIPTURE

We are now, and have been for the past two decades, living in what has been accurately called a post-Christian, postmodern world. The modern era was defined by the belief in and search for truth. The postmodern era leaves that belief behind and no longer recognizes absolute standards of morality or truth. Whatever feels right and does not "harm" others is considered acceptable behavior, and truth is what you feel it is. Defining truth in such an environment is a personal and subjective process.

But that viewpoint runs contrary to all we see in the natural and physical realms. Science—whether astronomy, zoology, botany, physiology, physics, or mathematics—is controlled by objective, fixed principles.

In terms of morality and worldview, however, the unsaved live by their own flexible standards, ignoring the existence of absolute laws in the spiritual realm. God incorporated moral laws into the fabric of life just as He established natural laws in the physical dimension. And people's not believing in such spiritual laws does not eliminate the negative consequences when they disobey them. One may choose not to believe in the law of gravity, but he will still fall to the ground if he jumps off a tower. Likewise, one may believe biblical moral standards are wrong or outmoded, but he or she cannot escape the consequences of violating those standards.

As believers, we know and respect the fact that God has absolute standards of morality, ethics, and truth. We also know He expects man to obey those standards. And of course the only reliable, authoritative source for God's unchanging rules for living is the Bible.

Armed with that knowledge and a Holy Spirit-given desire to obey (and with the assurance that God's Word is settled and sure; cf. Ps. 119:89; Matt. 24:35; 1 Pet. 1:25), we may confidently point unsaved family and friends to Scripture because it contains "the whole counsel of God concerning all things necessary for His own glory, man's salvation, faith and life" (Westminster Confession of Faith, chap. I, para. VI).

TESTIFYING TO AN INSPIRED WORD OF GOD

The first thing we need to proclaim and defend concerning Scripture is that it is a divinely inspired book. Inspiration was God's main way of revealing His message to mankind. The Holy Spirit made known to human writers the themes and words God wanted in the Old and New Testaments.

The Definition
This basic doctrine is spelled out most clearly in 2 Timothy 3:16: "All Scripture is inspired by God." The Greek word translated "inspired" is *theopneustos*, a compound word literally meaning "God-breathed." It refers to the entire content of the Bible—that which comes out of His mouth—His Word.

Inasmuch as God breathed the universe into existence (cf. Ps. 33:6), it makes sense that He also breathed the Bible into existence. Scriptures reflect the truth of whatever God has said. In some passages, the term *Scripture* is even synonymous with the name *God*: "The Scripture ... preached the gospel beforehand to Abraham, saying, 'All the nations shall be blessed in you'" (Gal. 3:8); "Scripture has shut up all men under sin, that the promise by faith in Jesus Christ might be given to those who believe" (v. 22). In those verses, the Bible speaks and acts as God's voice.

The same thing is true concerning other quotations of the Old Testament. The apostle Paul referred to God's speaking to Pharaoh (Exod. 9:16) when he wrote, "For the *Scripture says* to Pharaoh, 'For this very purpose I raised you up'" (Rom. 9:17, emphasis added). Whenever we read the Bible, we read God's words.

The Process

The truth of inspiration can still prompt the legitimate question, "How can the Bible be the Word of God and at the same time the words of the human writers?" The answer is, God the Holy Spirit formed and guided the thoughts and personalities of the men as they wrote. He made them into the persons He wanted them to be by controlling their heredity and shaping their environment. When in God's providence every factor in an author's life (personality, emotions, language skill, and so on) was just right, God oversaw the author's free choice so that he penned the very words and phrases God intended man to receive. We see evidence of that process when we read any book of the Bible. Each one has a unique character and varying literary style. We often sense the emotions the author had when he wrote the book. The words are men's words, but they are also God's words. It is therefore accurate to say that the Lord, through various men, wrote Scripture (cf. 2 Pet. 1:21).

The Extent

All Scripture is God-breathed. The word for "all" (*pasa*)—in the Greek it can also mean "every"—reinforces the fact that divine inspiration produced each and every word of Scripture.

Jesus implied that all of Scripture is inspired as a unified body of truth when He declared, "The Scripture cannot be broken" (John 10:35). The entire Bible is pure and authentic; *none* of its words can be nullified because they are all God's sacred writings (cf. 2 Tim. 3:15). Christ also stressed the divine significance of every small detail of Scripture when He said in His Sermon on the Mount, "For truly I say to you, until heaven and earth pass away, not the smallest letter or stroke shall pass away from the Law until all is accomplished" (Matt. 5:18). "Stroke" denotes a very small mark—about the size of punctuation marks in English—that was put under certain words. Man is not to tamper with God's Word; God views the matter that seriously. Every single part of Scripture is inspired, important, and worthy of our utmost respect.

GOD'S WORD: CONSIDERING THE FINAL PRODUCT

The Bible is God's inspired Word—not a mere collection of various writers' opinions, ideas, philosophies, or "inspired" thoughts. It is certainly not the result of a poll that asked what the public most wanted to hear or a compilation of the best insights from the world's greatest thinkers. Scripture is nothing less than the written revelation of God and as such possesses certain qualities that ought to be commended to anyone unsure about the claims of Christianity.

The Bible Is Infallible

First of all, it is important that we uphold to others the Bible's *infallibility*. A common affirmation of scriptural infallibility states, "The Bible is God's Word, the infallible rule of faith and practice." I believe that statement can and should be made even stronger: "The Bible is God's *infallible* Word, the only rule of faith and practice." Having the term *infallible* modify "Word" makes it unambiguous that we are asserting the Bible is infallible in its *entirety*. By this we mean that the original manuscripts, written by the inspired authors, were without mistakes. (Minor errors introduced into copies of Scripture over the centuries have been explained by competent, godly Bible scholars. And none of those mistakes by copyists has been serious enough to challenge Scripture's infallibility.)

The argument for the Word's infallibility is very logical. If a perfect God with perfect character is our ultimate authority, and if He inspired the writers of each book of Scripture, then each book is perfect (cf. Ps. 19:7; Prov. 30:5), and Scripture as a whole becomes our flawless, ultimate authority. Nothing else can legitimately replace it as a source for what people should believe and do.

The Bible Is Inerrant

Almost synonymous with biblical infallibility is the truth that the Bible is *inerrant*. The two concepts "have special value, for they explicitly safeguard crucial positive truths" ("The Chicago Statement on Biblical Inerrancy," International Council on Biblical Inerrancy, James M. Boice, chairman. Special conference on the authority of Scripture, Chicago, October 1978). The authors of "The Chicago Statement" further defined the two terms and indicated their important relationship in this way:

> *Infallible* signifies the quality of neither misleading nor being misled and so safeguards in categorical terms the truth that Holy Scripture is a sure, safe, and reliable rule and guide in all matters.
>
> Similarly, *inerrant* signifies the quality of being free from all falsehood or mistake and so safeguards the truth that Holy Scripture is entirely true and trustworthy in all its assertions. (emphases in original)

The term *truthfulness* accurately conveys the primary significance of infallibility and inerrancy. The Author of Scripture calls Himself the essence of truth (Isa. 65:16), and the prophet Jeremiah ascribes the same quality to Him: "The LORD is the true God" (Jer. 10:10). The writers of the New Testament also equated God with truth (e.g., John 3:33; 17:3; 1 John 5:20), and both Testaments emphasize that God does not lie (Num. 23:19; Titus 1:2; Heb. 6:18).

The Bible has to be inerrant because it is God's Word, and God is a God of truth. Proverbs 30:5 well summarizes the extent and practical implications of inerrancy: "Every word of God is tested [true]; He is a shield to those who take refuge in Him."

The Bible Is Authoritative

If the Bible is perfect and without error, it follows logically that we must present it as the most *authoritative* book in the world—the one document that contains the last word on truth. Bible interpreter

Robertson McQuilkin presents a most basic but compelling reason for anyone to accept Scripture as the final authority:

> Since God is the author, the Bible is authoritative. It is absolute in its authority for human thought and behavior. "As the Scripture has said" is a recurring theme throughout the New Testament. In fact, the New Testament contains more than two hundred direct quotations of the Old Testament. In addition, the New Testament has a large and uncertain number of allusions to the Old. New Testament writers, following the example of Jesus Christ, built their theology on the Old Testament. For Christ and the apostles, to quote the Bible was to settle an issue. (*Understanding and Applying the Bible* [Chicago: Moody Press, 1992], 20)

But unbelieving critics of Scripture led the departure from that high view of biblical authority. That movement really accelerated about the middle of the eighteenth century, during the Enlightenment period. Naturalistic presuppositions, human knowledge and reasoning, new scientific discoveries and theories, and more sophisticated insights from literature and philosophy were all used to "get at the real truth" of the Bible. All of that led to theological liberalism, in which so-called Bible scholars adopted a higher critical view of Scripture. Throughout the nineteenth century they increasingly saw the Bible as full of errors and myths, not written by the inspired apostles and prophets as claimed, and no more authoritative than the works of William Shakespeare or Charles Dickens.

In the early twentieth century neoorthodoxy arose as a response to some of the excesses of liberalism. Its advocates sought to restore Scripture's authority by reaffirming man's sinfulness and claiming that, although not *the* Word of God entirely, the Bible "contains" the Word of God.

But no genuine believers, or even discerning unbelievers, should be persuaded by neoorthodoxy. It still leaves us with a man-centered view of Scripture. The Bible becomes partly the Word of God and partly the word of man, and it is man's reason and presuppositions that act as final arbiters in determining what's authoritative and what's not.

The postmodern doubts and skepticism concerning the Bible are potential threats to everyone's relationship with God. If you give consideration to such assertions, you'll compromise your testimony and thus render it ineffective. And sadly, if unbelievers dismiss the Bible as just another book, they will, apart from the Spirit's intervention, forfeit any opportunity of repenting and believing the Gospel.

Consider the godly confidence in Scripture that nineteenth-century preacher C. H. Spurgeon possessed when he asserted, "There is no need for you to defend a lion when he's being attacked. All you need to do is open the gate and let him out."

The Bible Is Effective

One more quality that attests to the Bible's overall authenticity is its *effectiveness*. The prophet Isaiah, in picturesque language, describes Scripture's ability to bring the results God desires:

> *"For as the rain and the snow come down from heaven, and do not return there without watering the earth, and making it bear and sprout, and furnishing seed to the sower and bread to the eater; so shall My word be which goes forth from My mouth; it will not return to Me empty, without accomplishing what I desire, and without succeeding in the matter for which I sent it."*
>
> —Isa. 55:10-11

From time to time we experience the failure of some everyday product or device. Our cars and trucks break down along the road or even in our driveways. A necessary household appliance might not work because it wears out or there is a power outage. Even the most powerful, state-of-the-art laptop computer will not provide portable service if it has no power source or if its battery needs recharging. But we never need to have such worries regarding the Bible. It always works effectively and produces results in keeping with God's will (though not always according to man's schedule).

Paul expressed the effectiveness of the Bible in this way: "For our gospel did not come to you in word only, but also in power and in the Holy Spirit and with full conviction" (1 Thess. 1:5). When God's Word is proclaimed and defended, it goes forth with Spirit-generated power. And we can be assured that it will be effective.

THE BIBLE TESTIFIES TO ITSELF

In addition to the certain truths of the Bible's divine inspiration and its infallible authority and effectiveness, any faithful witness for Christ will want to defend what the Bible says about itself. We can appeal to three major sources that reliably demonstrate Scripture's consistency, unity, and authenticity: the human authors of the various books, the Lord Jesus Christ, and the divine Author, the Holy Spirit.

The Testimony of the Biblical Writers

The human writers through whom God's revelation was given came from diverse backgrounds. Paul was a Pharisee and theologian, Matthew a tax collector, Daniel a statesman, Luke a physician, Joshua a soldier. In addition, there were kings, priests, shepherds, and fishermen. Most of them were common and unassuming men without much formal education. It is truly amazing that, coming from such diversity and writing over a span of 1,600 years from far-flung locations, the Bible's authors uniformly wrote with a confidence that they were articulating the Word of God. Hundreds of times and in various ways they wrote with the same authority, composing a perfectly unified theme that always conveyed God's message infallibly.

The authors accurately dealt with many different areas of truth. They wrote about historical facts that can be verified. They made scientifically correct observations, such as Job 26:7, "He stretches out the north over empty space, and hangs the earth on nothing." Contemporary doctors acknowledge that the Bible's information on medicine and health can still help people today to live healthy lives.

Concerning some scientific facts, the Bible was actually way ahead of its time. In the sixteenth century English scientist William Harvey discovered how the human circulatory system works. But many centuries earlier the book of Leviticus stated, "The life of the flesh is in the blood" (17:11; cf. Gen. 9:4). Or consider the nineteenth-century English philosopher Herbert Spencer, who proposed five categories for the universe: time, force, action, space, and matter. But Moses opened the book of Genesis with this declaration: "In the beginning [time] God [force] created [action] the heavens [space] and the earth [matter]" (1:1).

The men who wrote Scripture could not possibly have obtained such insights solely by their own intellects. They had to have been writing God's words under His direction, and they testify to that fact many, many times throughout the Bible (more than 3,800 times in the Old Testament alone).

For example, the psalmist said, "The law of the LORD is perfect" (Ps. 19:7); "I wait for Thy word" (119:81); "Thy word is very pure" (119:140); "Thy law is truth" (119:142); "All Thy commandments are truth" (119:151); "Of old I have known from Thy testimonies that thou hast founded them forever" (119:152). The prophets too knew they were setting forth God's words, as Amos wrote: "Surely the LORD God does nothing unless He reveals His secret counsel to His servants the prophets" (Amos 3:7).

The New Testament writers wrote with an unshakable conviction that the Old Testament was God's Word (they quoted it more than 300 times). The apostle Paul told the Roman Christians, "For whatever was written in earlier times [the Old Testament] was written for our instruction, so that through perseverance and the encouragement of the Scriptures we might have hope" (Rom. 15:4). Peter also knew the Old Testament was divinely inspired: "No prophecy was ever made by an act of human will, but men moved by the Holy Spirit spoke from God" (2 Pet. 1:21). The writer of the book of Hebrews had the same understanding as Paul, Peter, and all the other New Testament authors: "God, after He spoke long ago to the fathers in the prophets in many portions and in many ways . . ." (Heb. 1:1).

The writings of Paul and Peter also correctly recognize that portions of the New Testament other than their own were from God. In one command to Timothy (1 Tim. 5:18), Paul implicitly ascribes divine authority to both the Old Testament and the words of Jesus in the Gospels: "For the Scripture says, 'You shall not muzzle the ox while he is threshing,' [Deut. 25:4] and 'The laborer is worthy of his wages' [Luke 10:7]." The apostle knew there was no higher authority than Scripture to support his teaching.

Later Peter offered one of the clearest statements in the Bible to attest that Paul's letters were inspired. Even though some Pauline passages are complex and difficult to interpret, Peter readily referred to his fellow apostle's writings to support his own teachings:

> *Regard the patience of our Lord to be salvation; just as also our beloved brother Paul, according to the wisdom given him, wrote to you, as also in all his letters, speaking in them of these things, in which are some things hard to understand, which the untaught and unstable distort, as they do also the rest of the Scriptures, to their own destruction.*
>
> —*2 Pet. 3:15-16*

With that statement, Peter also understood that Paul's writings had the utmost credibility and could accomplish the same objective as every other part of Scripture—namely, to instruct people in the plan and will of God.

The words of Paul and Peter and all the New Testament authors (e.g., the apostle John, see Rev. 19:9; 21:5), when taken as a whole, present a consistent testimony that respects the Old Testament as Scripture and understands that the New is also God's Word.

The Testimony of Jesus Christ

The second, and undoubtedly most credible, witness to the importance and authenticity of all Scripture is the Lord Jesus Christ. The Son of God disclosed that He was the central theme of the entire Bible: "You search the Scriptures, because you think that in them you have eternal life; and it is these that bear witness of Me" (John 5:39). And as the central focus of Scripture, Christ came to fulfill each and every part of it (cf. Matt. 5:17).

The primary way Jesus came to earth to fulfill Scripture was as the Messiah who would suffer, die, and rise from the dead for His people. Accordingly, He taught the two men on the road to Emmaus and later in the upper room:

> *"Was it not necessary for the Christ to suffer these things and to enter into His glory?" And beginning with Moses and with all the prophets, He explained to them the things concerning Himself in all the Scriptures. . . . "These are My words which I spoke to you while I was still with you, that all things which are written about Me in the Law of Moses and the Prophets and the Psalms must be fulfilled." Then He opened their minds to understand the Scriptures, and He said to them, "Thus it is written, that the Christ should suffer and rise again from the dead the third day, and that repentance for forgiveness of sins should be proclaimed in His name to all the nations, beginning from Jerusalem."*
> —Luke 24:26-27, 44-47; cf. Matt. 26:24, 54

When Christ taught, He always explicitly or implicitly supported the integrity of Scripture, as when He told the Jews, "The Scripture cannot be broken" (John 10:35). He meant that God's words were true and all that the Father had proclaimed through the Old Testament prophets would come to pass. In His omniscience, our Lord knew that Scripture was the written revelation of God and that nothing in the universe could thwart its accomplishment (cf. Luke 16:17; 18:31).

The Testimony of the Holy Spirit

As the Person of the Godhead who was involved in the process of biblical inspiration from start to finish, the Holy Spirit's role in witnessing to the veracity of Scripture is essentially to confirm the testimony of the writers and of the Lord Jesus Christ to those who believe.

Further, the Spirit is the one who empowers and confirms the truth as we proclaim God's Word to those outside of Christ.

No one we talk to will ever, simply by the power of human intellect, believe the Bible is the inspired Word of God. Just as in regeneration (John 3:5-8), in order for people to change their view toward Scripture, the Spirit must work in their lives. That sovereign work in the heart and mind will convince people that the Bible is from God, all its words are reliable, and it is the ultimate standard of morality and spiritual truth.

But unless believers are faithful to declare the Word, the Holy Spirit cannot do His internal work of convincing an individual that Scripture must be believed and obeyed from the heart. The apostle Paul's probing questions in Romans 10:14 must challenge us to defend and proclaim the truth whenever there is opportunity: "How then shall they call upon Him in whom they have not believed? How will they believe in Him whom they have not heard? And how will they hear without a preacher?"

Once the unsaved hear the Word of God, their depraved minds have an opportunity to receive the truth and be changed by it. If people are inclined to believe the Word (and often they will not be; cf. 1 Cor. 1:21-24), it will be the result of a supernatural change in their hearts. And that will occur as the Holy Spirit testifies to God's Word. Here's how Paul explained the crucial role of the Spirit in bringing the unregenerate to understand God's truth:

> For to us God revealed them [truths from Scripture] through the Spirit; for the Spirit searches all things, even the depths of God. For who among men knows the thoughts of a man except the spirit of the man, which is in him? Even so the thoughts of God no one knows except the Spirit of God. Now we have received, not the spirit of the world, but the Spirit who is from God, that we might know the things freely given to us by God, which things we also speak, not in words taught by human wisdom, but in those taught by the Spirit, combining spiritual thoughts with spiritual words. But a natural man does not accept the things of the Spirit of God;

for they are foolishness to him, and he cannot understand them,
because they are spiritually appraised. But he who is spiritual
appraises all things, yet he himself is appraised by no one. For who
has known the mind of the Lord, that he should instruct Him?
But we have the mind of Christ.

—1 Cor. 2:10-16

The Bible is a basic, indispensable tool for us as evangelists. Every time we proclaim and defend it before someone who is lost, we proclaim and defend God's truth. "Jesus therefore was saying to those Jews who had believed Him, 'If you abide in My word, then you are truly disciples of Mine; and you shall know the truth, and the truth shall make you free'" (John 8:31-32). Compare the meaning of Jesus' words to the end result of solving a mathematical equation or doing a scientific experiment. When the calculations are successfully completed or the experiment leads to a new discovery, there is a great sense of freedom and relief for the mathematician or scientist who finds the answer.

Men and women search and struggle for the truth in life and are determined to keep looking until it is revealed to them. We as Christians have the privilege of pointing them to the source of truth and genuine spiritual freedom, the Bible. Once they by faith embrace God's Word, they will see that it says all they really need to know about God, mankind, life, death, right, wrong, husbands, wives, children—all that's necessary for dealing with life's important issues. They can trust the Bible because it's God's living Word.

Chapter 6

Amazing Prophecies

We have just seen in the previous chapter the crucial importance of defending and proclaiming the Bible as a divinely inspired, inerrant, authentic, and authoritative book. Such reliance upon the trustworthiness of Scripture is certainly vital in any sound evangelistic approach. But an additional feature of divine revelation that is invaluable as a tool in declaring Christianity's validity is fulfilled prophecy. Henry Morris correctly states the case this way:

> An especially powerful type of historical evidence [for the Bible and Christianity] is that of fulfilled prophecy—historical events written down long before they actually happen. Hundreds of prophecies in the Bible have been remarkably fulfilled exactly as foretold but often hundreds of years later. This type of evidence is unique to the Bible and can be explained only by divine inspiration. God, the Creator of time, is outside of time. He is the One who controls the future and, therefore, is the only One who knows the future.
>
> Bible prophecies are not vague and rambling, such as those of Nostradamus and other supposed extrabiblical prophets. Prophecies in the Bible deal with specific places, people, and events, and their fulfillments can be checked by reference to subsequent history. (*Science and the Bible* [Chicago: Moody Press, 1986], 117)

CHARACTERISTICS OF PROPHECY

Scripture is the product of the God who knows everything. Therefore its various accounts of prewritten history were composed with absolute precision. We can see that precision as we examine four characteristics of predictive prophecy: its definition, its standards, its scope, and its distinctiveness.

Prophecy's Definition

Men and women can have certain insights into the past based on a study of history. But human insights into the future are much more tenuous. Various indicators allow us to foresee business, political, and social trends and enable us to forecast the weather with greater and greater accuracy. But no mortal can predict future events in exact detail. Only God can make those kinds of predictions, and He did so numerous times through the prophets of Scripture.

Genuine predictive prophecy is a revelation of God, not merely an almost-accurate guess or a wise bit of speculation. Such prophecy is a statement of historical fact, made in advance, which is beyond the scope of any human capability. God told the prophet Isaiah, "I am God, and there is no other; I am God, and there is no one like Me, declaring the end from the beginning, and from ancient times things which have not been done" (Isa. 46:9-10). The Lord alone is omniscient, and so only His Word can predict the future with absolute accuracy.

Prophecy's Divine Standard

In very straightforward terms God told the prophet Jeremiah what His basic standard for true prophecy was: "The prophet who prophesies of peace, when the word of the prophet shall come to pass, then that prophet will be known as one whom the LORD has truly sent" (Jer. 28:9; cf. Isa. 41:21-23). The prophet who is from God will predict the future with total accuracy.

Centuries earlier, God instructed Moses concerning His strict standard of prophetic credibility:

> "'But the prophet who shall speak a word presumptuously in My name which I have not commanded him to speak, or which he shall speak in the name of other gods, that prophet shall die.' You

may say in your heart, 'How shall we know the word which the LORD has not spoken?' When a prophet speaks in the name of the LORD, if the thing does not come about or come true, that is the thing which the LORD has not spoken. The prophet has spoken it presumptuously; you shall not be afraid of him."

—*Deut. 18:20-22*

If just one Bible prophecy departed from God's standard of perfect accuracy, all of His Word would be susceptible to allegations of error.

The Scope of Prophecy

The Bible contains prophetic verses and passages throughout its pages. For instance, the first prophecy about Christ and the Gospel appears as early as Genesis 3:15, when God said to the serpent in the Garden of Eden, "And I will put enmity between you and the woman, and between your seed and her seed; he shall bruise you on the head, and you shall bruise him on the heel." The seed of the woman (Mary) was Jesus Christ, and the head of the serpent was Satan. Of course, the fulfillment of this prophecy was the death and resurrection of Christ.

Many other portions of the Old Testament are also prophetic, including twenty chapters in Isaiah, seventeen chapters in Jeremiah, nine chapters in Ezekiel, and two chapters in Amos. Those prophecies are quite diverse in subject and scope, some relating to individuals, others to large groups of people. Some of the pronouncements are directed at individual cities, others to entire nations, and some to the whole world.

Out of all the diversity of prophecy's scope, the focal point and supreme example of its fulfillment was the incarnation of Jesus Christ. That immense miracle, along with His earthly ministry, death, and resurrection, was the consummation of all that the Old Testament prophets wrote. When John the Baptist sent some of his disciples to ask Jesus if He was the promised Messiah, the Lord answered by alluding to His fulfillment of messianic prophecy (see Matt. 11:2-6).

The Distinctiveness of Prophecy

Biblical prophecy was distinctive in that it often went beyond the comprehension of the human prophets who spoke and wrote it. That's because many of the prophecies, coming from a divine perspective, seemed so incongruous with contemporary situations and unlikely ever to be fulfilled (e.g., the destruction of powerful Babylon). But this feature of prophecy simply confirms again its supernatural character—it had to be from an omniscient, omnipotent God, not from the fallible minds of the prophets themselves.

Although the prophets foretold many events, they often did not grasp how God would orchestrate in detail the fulfillment of those prophecies. For example, 1 Peter 1:10-11 shows that those who wrote of Messiah tried to understand what person and time they were actually writing about. Yet those men were faithful instruments in recording God's inspired, completely accurate prophecies. Two examples illustrate the point.

The prophet Isaiah indicated that King Cyrus of Persia would release the Jews from captivity and allow them to return to Jerusalem and rebuild its walls, which that king did in 538 B.C.—"It is I [God] who says of Cyrus, 'He is My shepherd! And he will perform all My desire.' And he declares of Jerusalem, 'She will be built,' and of the temple, 'Your foundation will be laid'" (Isa. 44:28). Isaiah uttered those words at least a century before Cyrus was even born!

An unnamed prophet confronted Jeroboam and "cried against the altar by the word of the LORD, and said, 'O altar, altar, thus says the LORD, "Behold, a son shall be born to the house of David, Josiah by name; and on you he shall sacrifice the priests of the high places who burn incense on you, and human bones shall be burned on you"'" (1 Kings 13:2). Three hundred years before Josiah was born, God said he would destroy the illegitimate priests of the high places who made improper offerings on the altar at Bethel. That prophecy was fulfilled in 2 Kings 23:15-20. Seven hundred years before Jesus was born, the prophet Micah predicted it would be in Bethlehem (5:2).

The major characteristics of predictive prophecy unquestionably affirm the reliability of Scripture and its validity as a tool in proclaiming and defending God's truth. Our use of the Bible will sometimes be put to the test—and for the vast majority of true Christians, it already has been. But a careful, fair-minded examination of fulfilled prophecy—the examples in this chapter and others too numerous to discuss—always vindicates the Bible's claims, especially the truth of Christ and His Gospel.

TWO AMAZING FULFILLED PROPHECIES

The Christian faith is based on genuine historical events. Jesus lived, died, and rose again in history. The Bible also has many other references to historical names, places, and events. Many of these, as we've already indicated, are contained within the context of prophecy, or "prewritten" history. Scripture predicted that the Phoenician city of Tyre would eventually cease to exist, and it did. Scripture said the great city of Babylon would fall, and it did. In both instances the fulfilled prophecies were verified by the record of history and modern archaeology.

I believe a closer look at each of the two aforementioned examples will further convince us what an incredible, powerful instrument Scripture is in affirming God's truth to those who may yet be unconvinced, or simply uninformed.

The Prophecy Concerning Tyre

Tyre was one of the largest, most powerful cities of ancient Phoenicia, which is modern-day Lebanon. A large wall protected Tyre's citizens from invasions by land, and their famous naval fleet protected them from attack by sea.

Tyre was already flourishing during Joshua's time. Later its king, Hiram, offered David cedars to build his royal palace and loaned him artisans to craft parts of the new structure (1 Chron. 14:1). Similarly,

Hiram (or Huram) later supplied cedar timber to help Solomon build the temple (2 Chron. 2:16).

In spite of its stature as the commercial center of the Mediterranean in Old Testament times (see Ezek. 27:3) and its previously good relationship with David and Solomon, Tyre was among the seven nations in Ezekiel 25:1—32:32 that God directed the prophet to proclaim judgment against. Ezekiel 26—28 is devoted to the pronouncement against Tyre, with these specific predictions highlighted in chapter 26:

- Many nations would invade Tyre, coming against it like successive waves of the sea (vv. 3-4).
- King Nebuchadnezzar of Babylon would destroy the mainland portion of the city (vv. 7-8).
- The city would be turned into a flat rock (vv. 4, 14).
- The fishermen would dry their nets on that rock (vv. 5, 14).
- The rubble of the city would be thrown into the sea (v. 12).
- Tyre would never be rebuilt (v. 14).

All of those prophetic details were perfectly fulfilled in history. Not long after Ezekiel's reference to Nebuchadnezzar, the king of Babylon did exactly what had been predicted—he laid siege to the city of Tyre in 585 B.C. After thirteen years of blockading the city, the Babylonians broke through its gates but found that most of the residents had fled.

During the long siege, Tyre's citizens had moved all their possessions a half mile by ship to an offshore island fortress. Although Nebuchadnezzar ruined the mainland city (Ezek. 26:8), he obtained no plunder (29:17-20), and the new offshore city continued for another 250 years. Further, Ezekiel 26:12, which says, "Also they will . . . throw your stones and your timbers and your debris into the water," would remain unfulfilled for the time being. But it was eventually fulfilled in 332 B.C. during Alexander the Great's campaign to conquer the known world. The Greek ruler's army had already defeated the Persians and was pushing southward toward Egypt.

When his forces arrived in Phoenicia, Alexander ordered the cities to open their gates to him. However, Tyre refused and rested in the security of its island location and the strength of its fleet.

Alexander knew he could not match Tyre's naval prowess; so he directed his men to use the rubble from the mainland city to build a 200-foot-wide causeway to the island city. After they tossed chunks of debris into the water, they leveled the material to form a usable causeway. (To fend off the nearly steady barrage of Tyrian missiles, the Greeks used mobile shields as they worked.) The entire operation was the beginning of the literal fulfillment of Ezekiel 26:12.

Because of the relentless resistance from Tyre, Alexander finally realized he would need ships to protect his forces' flanks. Therefore he compelled support from the previously conquered cities to help him finish the campaign against Tyre. That fulfilled God's words in Ezekiel 26:3-4.

Alexander victoriously concluded his seven-month effort against Tyre. His 160-foot-high mobile siege towers, along with the naval reinforcements, mounted a devastating final assault that overpowered the walls of Tyre. In addition to the many killed in battle, 30,000 Tyrians were sold into slavery.

Tyre never regained its prominence and prestige. The island portion of the city was repopulated for a while but was destroyed by the Muslims in A.D. 1281. However, precisely according to God's Word (Ezek. 26:14, "You will be built no more"), the mainland site has not been rebuilt. Even nineteenth-century historians pointed out that much of the ancient site is now barren rock, used by fishermen to dry their nets. That situation fulfills the prophecies of Ezekiel 26:4-5.

All the events related to the demise of Tyre demonstrate that biblical prophecy is an infallible guide to history. No human observer could have looked down the corridor of time and foreseen the permanent destruction of a powerful city like Tyre.

The Prophecy Concerning Babylon

Babylon was one of the greatest cities of the ancient world. It was founded 1,800 years before Christ by Hammurabi. However, it reached its height of power and prestige under Nabopolasser and his son Nebuchadnezzar in the seventh and sixth centuries B.C. It was the capital of the Babylonian (Chaldean) Empire and was noted for its great wealth and its high level of culture and education. The city was also very advanced commercially and had beautiful, sophisticated architecture that was much admired in the ancient world.

Nineteenth-century archaeological finds first helped contemporary observers appreciate the splendor of ancient Babylon. Prior to those discoveries, the city's site was so desolate that no one was sure where it was located. We now know that the Euphrates River ran through the middle and under the walls of Babylon and that the city was in the midst of a marshy area.

The famous Greek historian Herodotus, who lived and wrote less than a century after Babylon was destroyed, recorded (*Histories* 1:181) that the city occupied a 196-square-mile area and was surrounded by a wide moat. It was further protected by a fifty-six-mile-long wall that was 311 feet high and eighty-seven feet wide. That wall had a total of 100 bronze gates.

The prophets Isaiah and Jeremiah predicted the destruction of Babylon and the accompanying environmental aftereffects (see Isa. 13:3—14:23, especially 13:19-22; 14:23; Jer. 50:1—51:58, especially 51:26, 43). They included specific facts about the ruins of Babylon that were later verified: certain animals would be there, the Arabs would not pitch their tents on the site, and the location would remain desolate and uninhabited.

Herodotus (*Histories* 1:190-192) reported on the political and military factors involved in Babylon's demise. As a prestigious and strategically important city, the Persians coveted control of Babylon. Their army, however, realized that under existing conditions it could not overcome the well-fortified city. Therefore, the Persians calculated that the Euphrates' riverbed was deep enough and wide enough for their forces to march through. The commanders thus ordered the troops to divert river water from Babylon by means of huge canals. Digging such channels drained the riverbed and allowed the Persian army to march across and storm the city.

The Babylonian leaders felt so secure behind the city walls that while the Persians were attacking, they held a drunken party. The book of Daniel takes a detailed look at that party and provides us with God's perspective on the immorality, idolatry, and general sinfulness that resulted in Babylon's fall. Here's how the prophet Daniel described it:

Belshazzar the king held a great feast for a thousand of his nobles, and he was drinking wine in the presence of the thousand. When Belshazzar tasted the wine, he gave orders to bring the gold and silver vessels which Nebuchadnezzar his father had taken out of the temple which was in Jerusalem, so that the king and his nobles, his wives and his concubines might drink from them. Then they brought the gold vessels that had been taken out of the temple, the house of God which was in Jerusalem; and the king and his nobles, his wives and his concubines drank from them. They drank the wine and praised the gods of gold and silver, of bronze, iron, wood and stone. Suddenly the fingers of a man's hand emerged and began writing opposite the lampstand on the plaster of the wall of the king's palace, and the king saw the back of the hand that did the writing. Then the king's face grew pale and his thoughts alarmed him, and his hip joints went slack, and his knees began knocking together. The king called aloud to bring in the conjurers, the Chaldeans and the diviners. The king spoke and said to the wise men of Babylon, "Any man who can read this inscription and explain its interpretation to me shall be clothed with purple, and have a necklace of gold around his neck, and have authority as third ruler in the kingdom." Then all the king's wise men came in, but they could not read the inscription or make known its interpretation to the king. Then King Belshazzar was greatly alarmed, his face grew even paler, and his nobles were perplexed. The queen entered the banquet hall because of the words of the king and his nobles; the queen spoke and said, "O king, live forever! Do not let your thoughts alarm you or your face be pale. There is a man in your kingdom in whom is a spirit of the holy gods; and in the days of your father, illumination, insight and wisdom like the wisdom of the gods were found in him. And King Nebuchadnezzar, your father, your father the king, appointed him chief of the magicians, conjurers, Chaldeans, and diviners. This was because an extraordinary spirit, knowledge and insight, interpretation of dreams, explanation of enigmas, and solving of difficult problems were found in this Daniel, whom the king named Belteshazzar. Let Daniel now be summoned and he will declare the interpretation." . . .

Then Daniel answered and said before the king, "Keep your gifts for yourself or give your rewards to someone else; however, I will read the inscription to the king and make the interpretation known to him. O king, the Most High God granted sovereignty, grandeur, glory, and majesty to Nebuchadnezzar your father. Because of the grandeur which He bestowed on him, all the peoples, nations, and men of every language feared and trembled before him; whomever he wished he killed, and whomever he wished he spared alive; and whomever he wished he elevated, and whomever he wished he humbled. But when his heart was lifted up and his spirit became so proud that he behaved arrogantly, he was deposed from his royal throne, and his glory was taken away from him. He was also driven away from mankind, and his heart was made like that of beasts, and his dwelling place was with the wild donkeys. He was given grass to eat like cattle, and his body was drenched with the dew of heaven, until he recognized that the Most High God is ruler over the realm of mankind, and that He sets over it whomever He wishes. Yet you, his son, Belshazzar, have not humbled your heart, even though you knew all this, but you have exalted yourself against the Lord of heaven; and they have brought the vessels of His house before you, and you and your nobles, your wives and your concubines have been drinking wine from them; and you have praised the gods of silver and gold, of bronze, iron, wood and stone, which do not see, hear or understand. But the God in whose hand are your life-breath and your ways, you have not glorified. Then the hand was sent from Him and this inscription was written out. Now this is the inscription that was written out: 'MENE, MENE, TEKEL,

*UPHARSIN.' This is the interpretation of the message:
'MENE'—God has numbered your kingdom and put an end
to it. 'TEKEL'—you have been weighed on the scales and found
deficient. 'PERES'—your kingdom has been divided and given
over to the Medes and Persians." Then Belshazzar gave orders,
and they clothed Daniel with purple and put a necklace of gold
around his neck, and issued a proclamation concerning him that
he now had authority as the third ruler in the kingdom. That
same night Belshazzar the Chaldean king was slain. So Darius
the Mede received the kingdom at about the age of sixty-two.*
—*Dan. 5:1-12, 17-31*

Those momentous events occurred around 539 B.C. Today the
windswept ruins of Babylon lie forty-five miles south of Baghdad.
Archaeologist Kerman Kilprect observed in *Explorations in Bible Lands
in the Nineteenth Century*, "What a contrast between the ancient civi-
lization and the modern degradation. Wild animals, boars, and hye-
nas, jackals, and wolves, and an occasional lion infest the jungle [site
of ancient Babylon]" (cited in George Davis, *Bible Prophecies Fulfilled
Today* [Philadelphia: Million Testaments Campaign], 1955, 78-79).
That is precisely what Isaiah prophesied in 13:19-22 and 14:23. The
area is now so desolate and inhospitable (most of the region is buried
under a deep layer of silt) that the Bedouins won't live there.
Vegetation doesn't grow there because the soil is so poor.

Statistician Peter Stoner, commenting on Jeremiah's prediction
that "They will not take from you even a stone for a corner" (51:26),
pointed out that the "rocks, which were imported to Babylon at such
great cost, have never been moved" (*Science Speaks: An Evaluation of
Certain Christian Evidences* [Chicago: Moody Press, 1963], 94). The
prophet also said men would not pass by Babylon's ruins (51:43), and
today there is no road leading there, and few people visit the site.

The probability that all those prophecies about Babylon were fulfilled merely by chance or coincidence is approximately one in five
billion—which is essentially *no* chance (Stoner, *Science Speaks*, 95).

God destroyed the city, and the results remain to this day, just as indicated in the amazing prophecies of the Old Testament.

Only an all-powerful, all-knowing, sovereign God could, through the prophets of Scripture, speak of events long before they happened and have the absolute confidence that His words were completely accurate and would be 100 percent fulfilled. The uncanny accuracy of fulfilled prophecy supports the reliability and supernatural character of the Bible. Erroneous prophetic statements, even if there were only one or two, would certainly undermine the truth of God's Word and ruin believers' testimony to an already-skeptical world.

Just as the amazing prophecies we have examined in this chapter—and many others in Scripture we could have discussed—can be trusted, so can the Lord's statements on *all* basic doctrines. The Bible says God created the heavens and the earth in six days, and He did. It says Jesus is the Son of God, and He is. And finally, God's Word says salvation comes only through faith in the substitutionary death of Jesus Christ on the cross, and it does. Fulfilled prophecy is truly a powerful tool we can use in sharing the Gospel.

Chapter 7

THE REALITY OF SIN

J. Wilbur Chapman, well-known evangelist and Bible conference director of a century ago, told the story of a prominent Australian preacher who once spoke very strongly on the subject of sin. After that service, one of the officers in his church came to the pastor's study and admonished him, saying, "Dr. Howard, we don't want you to talk as openly as you do about man's corruption, because if our boys and girls hear you discussing the subject, they will more easily become sinners. Call it a mistake if you will, but don't speak so plainly about sin."

The pastor took down a small bottle from a cabinet and showed it to the man.

"Do you see that label?" the pastor asked. "It says *strychnine*, and underneath in bold red letters is the word *poison*. Do you know, sir, what you are asking me to do? You're suggesting that I change the label. Suppose I do and paste over it the words *essence of peppermint*. Do you see what might happen? Someone would use it not knowing the danger involved and would die—and so it is too with the matter of sin. The milder you make the label, the more dangerous you make the poison."

That story illustrates well the serious task every witness for Jesus Christ has. If we are to be faithful and meticulous witnesses and evangelists, we must proclaim and defend even the unpleasant doctrines of Scripture. That means we cannot sidestep the doctrine of man's sin nor mitigate the spiritual dangers sin poses. Instead, we must speak of the subject in accord with God's Word.

Chrysostom, the early church father, said, "I fear nothing but sin." That's exactly how I feel. I fear nothing in the world or the church except sin. And Christians should all feel that way because of the terrible consequences that sin produces. It is the greatest problem facing mankind, the one great blight that curses us all. As a result of sin, the world has warfare between nations, conflict between individuals and groups, fear and anxiety, illness and death, and all kinds of natural and man-made disasters.

Genesis 3—4 report that the curse of sin after the Fall disrupted three basic relationships. First, men and women were separated from God when they became subject to spiritual death (Gen. 3:6-13; cf. 2:17). Second, they became at odds with nature. From then on it would resist their efforts to cultivate and control it (Gen. 3:17-19). Third, people were separated from each other as sin brought envy and conflict into the world, as exemplified by the strife between Cain and Abel (Gen. 4:3-15). Everyone who dies, no matter from what cause, dies as a victim of sin. Romans 6:23 says, "The wages of sin is death." Thus every human being is subject to the fearful power of sin.

SIN: ITS DEFINITION

Anything as severe as sin needs a definition so people can understand it and know why they need to be free from it. The definition is simple: "sin is lawlessness" (1 John 3:4). The Greek construction of this phrase makes "sin" and "lawlessness" identical. Literally it says everyone doing sin is doing lawlessness. Practicing sin is living as if there were no God and no law. It is arrogantly living on one's own terms, not being bound by God's standards.

Scripture also contains other definitions of sin. One of these is *unrighteousness*, as 1 John 5:17 says: "All unrighteousness is sin." Another is *the failure to do good*: "Therefore, to one who knows the right thing to do, and does not do it, to him it is sin" (Jas. 4:17). And finally, the apostle Paul defines sin as *a lack of faith*: "whatever is not from faith is sin" (Rom. 14:23).

But sin is still best identified as the equivalent of lawlessness— ignoring God's Law and going outside the boundaries He has set for us. Mankind is like a horse in a lush pasture that jumps the surrounding hedge and lands in a quagmire on the other side. Similarly, people are exposed to God's perfect and holy Law; but they want to get away, so they jump the fence of God's Law and land in the muck of sin.

God has revealed His Law in Scripture and has written it on man's heart: "When Gentiles who do not have the Law do instinctively the things of the Law, these, not having the Law, are a law to themselves, in that they show the work of the Law written in their hearts, their conscience bearing witness, and their thoughts alternately accusing or else defending them" (Rom. 2:14-15). Because God's Law is "holy and righteous and good" (Rom. 7:12), it is irrational to break it and forfeit the blessings obedience brings. But men and women, because of their sin, break the Law of God and often seek to live as far apart from it as they can.

SIN: ITS CHARACTERISTICS

The Bible spells out in considerable detail the major characteristics of sin. For the following four traits, the authors of Scripture use such graphic terms and clear analogies that it's difficult not to recognize what sin entails.

The Defilement of Sin

Sin is not only a flouting of God's Law, but also a defiling or polluting of the divine standard. It is to the soul what scars are to a beautiful face, what a dark stain is to a white silk cloth, or what black soot is to a clear blue sky. Sin makes a person's soul red with guilt and unrighteousness. By the use of stark terminology from the human and physical realm, the Old Testament indelibly impresses on our minds the horrible nature of sin's defilement.

The prophet Isaiah perhaps captures most vividly just how bad sin's defilement is in God's eyes: "Then you will defile your idols overlaid with silver and your images covered with gold; you will throw them away like a menstrual cloth" (Isa. 30:22, NIV). Isaiah compares the sin of idolatry to the bloody cloth used during a woman's menstrual period.

The writer of 1 Kings compares the sin of an individual's heart with a deadly plague of disease: "each knowing the affliction of his own heart" (8:38). The prophet Zechariah uses the figure of "filthy garments" on the high priest Joshua to depict the defilement of sin (Zech. 3:3).

Ezekiel notes that sin's defilement is so great that when the repentant sinner sees his sin he will actually hate himself: "There you will remember your ways and all your deeds, with which you have defiled yourselves; and you will loathe yourselves in your own sight for all the evil things that you have done" (Ezek. 20:43).

The Bible's overall impression of sin is that it's vile, wretched, and filthy, polluting everything that is pure. The apostle Paul uses these words as he urges believers to cleanse their lives of sin's terrible effects: "Let us cleanse ourselves from all defilement of flesh and spirit, perfecting holiness in the fear of God" (2 Cor. 7:1).

The Rebellion of Sin

Sin also involves rebellion against God. Scripture describes those who rebel as people who walk contrary to God and defy Him (Lev. 26:27). If sinners had their way, they would go as far as overthrowing God, which is what Satan attempted to do (cf. Isa. 14:12-21).

The rebellion of sin also includes the sinner's trampling on God's Law and being an affront to God by in a sense slapping Him in the face (that's what soldiers actually did to Jesus at His trial). Hebrews 10:29 indicates God's strong displeasure toward those who consider the truth and then sinfully reject it: "How much severer punishment do you think he will deserve who has trampled under foot the Son of God, and has regarded as unclean the blood of the covenant by which he was sanctified, and has insulted the Spirit of grace?"

Sin is nothing less than open, flagrant rebellion against God and His Word. Those who practice sin are essentially saying, "We'll do exactly what we want!"

The Ingratitude of Sin

God created men and women to praise and glorify Him forever, which is a loftier purpose than they could ever imagine on their own.

Everyone owes his very existence and all that he has to God (Acts 17:28), and yet multitudes of people live each day in absolute ingratitude.

If there is any joy for people in everyday life, it is because God gave it to them. Everything good that men and women are and have is the result of God's merciful common grace that He has revealed to all (Rom. 1:19-20). In the Sermon on the Mount Jesus told His disciples, "He causes His sun to rise on the evil and the good, and sends rain on the righteous and the unrighteous" (Matt. 5:45). God has provided all the food, shelter, and clothing the unbeliever enjoys. He has given men their senses so that they might appreciate a world of color and brightness, the sounds of music and laughter, the aroma of good food and the scent of fresh flowers, and all the other benefits that make life worth living. God also grants us the emotions and intellect to think, feel, work, play, and interact with other people so that we may live productive and useful lives. In spite of all these mercies, however, men and women still rebel against the Law of God and live with flagrant ingratitude toward all He has given them.

Unbelievers often indulge themselves in God's common grace, selfishly accepting the good things life has to offer and yet turning away from God and serving Satan instead. Such ingratitude is illustrated by Absalom who, after his father David had kissed and embraced him, went out and plotted treason against his father (see 2 Sam. 15:7—17:4). Sin is such gross ingratitude that it seeks to dethrone and destroy God, who is the source of everything good. Even the privileges people should be most thankful for—a comfortable standard of living, marital pleasures, and family relationships—they distort and pervert, and thereby dishonor God.

The Incurableness of Sin

With sin, man has a horrible, pervasive, incurable spiritual disease that cannot be defeated by human means (cf. Jer. 13:23). Isaiah depicted the nature of Israel's sin by comparing it to a set of physical ailments:

"Alas, sinful nation, people weighed down with iniquity, offspring of evildoers, sons who act corruptly! They have abandoned the LORD, they have despised the Holy One of Israel, they have turned away from Him. Where will you be stricken again, as you continue in your rebellion? The whole head is sick, and the whole heart is faint. From the sole of the foot even to the head there is nothing sound in it, only bruises, welts, and raw wounds, not pressed out or bandaged, nor softened with oil."

—1:4-6

Men and women in their own strength cannot cure the sin that is within them because their minds and consciences are defiled and depraved (cf. Rom. 1:24-32; Titus 1:15). The Puritan John Flavel wrote, "All the tears of a penitent sinner, should he shed as many as there have fallen drops of rain since the creation, cannot wash away sin! The everlasting burnings in hell cannot purify the flaming conscience from the least sin." There is simply no human remedy for the problem of sin. It will not be cured by any acts of human will, any programs of moral reformation or educational renewal, no pieces of legislation, no efforts of man-made counseling and consultation, nor any deeds of self-righteousness.

Sin is a deep-seated, terminal disease that can be cured only by the healing work of the Great Physician. The writer of Hebrews says this about the contrast between insufficient remedies for sin and God's perfect cure in Jesus Christ: "Every priest stands daily ministering and offering time after time the same sacrifices, which can never take away sins; but He [Christ], having offered one sacrifice for sins for all time, sat down at the right hand of God, waiting from that time onward until His enemies be made a footstool for His feet. For by one offering He has perfected for all time those who are sanctified" (10:11-14; cf. 9:11-14).

For all the pain sin causes, it's amazing how hard many unsaved people work at doing it (cf. Ps. 7:14; Prov. 4:16; Jer. 9:5; Ezek. 24:12). It brings them a certain sense of temporary enjoyment, but ultimately it leads to grief, death, and eternal hell. Such people may work hard at sinning, but we can offer them Jesus' promise of relief: "Come to Me, all who are weary and heavy-laden, and I will give you rest" (Matt. 11:28). People need relief from the evil characteristics of sin, and that relief can come only through the work of Christ.

SIN: ITS EXTENT

The book of Romans clearly states that sin's extent is universal. Just a few verses make that quite clear: "For we have already charged that both Jews and Greeks are all under sin; as it is written, 'There is none righteous, not even one; there is none who understands, there is none who seeks for God; all have turned aside, together they have become useless; there is none who does good, there is not even one'" (3:9-12). "For all have sinned and fall short of the glory of God" (3:23). "Therefore, just as through one man [Adam] sin entered into the world, and death through sin, and so death spread to all men, because all sinned . . ." (5:12).

That last verse says that not only was the guilt of Adam's sin imputed to every person, but the depravity and corruption of his nature was also transmitted to everyone. It's similar to the transmission of contaminated water: the poison goes from the spring to the well to the people who drink. Theologians call this reality *original sin*.

When we enter this world, we are already sinners. Sin is in our natures, woven into the very fabric of our lives (cf. Ps. 51:5). That's because we are all descendants of Adam, and as such, we all bear his corruption. Adam's sin clings to each one of us, just as Naaman's leprosy clung to Gehazi (2 Kings 5:27). And we who are believers know from experience that even after one is saved, the deep-seated nature of sin is still present. Therefore, we struggle like the apostle Paul, who wrote, "For the good that I want, I do not do; but I practice the very evil that I do not wish . . . but I see a different law in the members of my body, waging war against the law of my mind, and making me a prisoner of the law of sin which is in my members" (Rom. 7:19, 23).

The writer of the book of Hebrews, sent to Jewish believers, undoubtedly understood the principle Paul spoke of: "Let us also lay aside every encumbrance, and the sin which so easily entangles us, and let us run with endurance the race that is set before us" (12:1). Why are we so easily entangled with sin? Because without exception, sin is a part of our natures; none of us escapes.

SIN: ITS RESULTS

Scripture contains abundant teaching on the dominant results of sin in individuals' lives. It controls the mind, the will, the affections, and ultimately the person's entire being. The minds of unbelievers are dominated by evil (Jer. 17:9; Eph. 4:17-19); and because of sin, they cannot understand spiritual truth (1 Cor. 2:14).

Sin controls not only what people think, but also what they decide to do and what they come to love. Jeremiah 44:16-17 is a lesser-known example of how sin can cause people to willfully reject God's words. The Jews in Egypt wanted nothing to do with the prophet's message: "As for the message that you have spoken to us in the name of the LORD, we are not going to listen to you! But rather we will certainly carry out every word that has proceeded from our mouths."

The apostle John perhaps made the definitive statements on the domineering effect sin has on the affections of men and women. Even believers can love the wrong things or love things the wrong way: "Do not love the world, nor the things in the world. If any one loves the world, the love of the Father is not in him. For all that is in the world, the lust of the flesh and the lust of the eyes and the boastful pride of life, is not from the Father, but is from the world" (1 John 2:15-16). John's Gospel recorded Jesus' words concerning the complete domination that sin has on the hearts of the unregenerate: "This is the judgment, that the light has come into the world, and men loved the darkness rather than the light; for their deeds were evil" (John 3:19).

Implicit in such domination by sin is that all people are also under the control of Satan until they come to Christ: "And you were dead in your trespasses and sins, in which you formerly walked according to the course of this world, according to the prince of the power of the air [Satan], of the spirit that is now working in the sons of disobedience" (Eph. 2:1-2). Under Satan's dominion, there is no freedom but only slavery (cf. John 8:44; Rom. 6:16; 1 John 5:19).

The apostle Paul goes on in Ephesians 2 to identify those controlled by their sin nature as "children of wrath" (v. 3). That makes them the ideal targets for God's judgment, the objects of the wrath of a God who hates sin. Jesus identified all unbelievers as objects of God's wrath: "He who does not obey the Son shall not see life, but the wrath of God abides on him" (John 3:36; cf. 1 Cor. 16:22; Gal. 3:10).

Sinners who live under God's wrath are much like Damocles who, according to the old story, sat eating at a banquet table while a sword suspended by a thin thread hung over his head. Even with that immediate danger, Damocles went on eating. Likewise, the sword of God's wrath hangs over the heads of unbelievers; yet so many continue on through life eating, drinking, and having fun, oblivious to their spiritual need. That situation ought to prompt us to proclaim, in the spirit of John the Baptist, the only salvation from divine wrath—the Gospel (Matt. 3:7-12; Luke 3:7-9; cf. 1 Thess. 1:10).

As if it weren't bad enough that man's fall into sin subjected him and the whole creation to many miseries and hardships (Gen. 3:8-24; Job 5:7; Eccl. 1:2; Rom. 8:18-22), the most devastating result of sin is that it can damn the soul to eternal punishment and separation from God in hell. The apostle John saw this awesomely frightening vision of the great white throne judgment and what will be the eternal destiny of all who die unrepentant in their sins:

And I saw a great white throne and Him who sat upon it, from whose presence earth and heaven fled away, and no place was found for them. And I saw the dead, the great and the small, standing before the throne, and books were opened; and another book was opened, which is the book of life; and the dead were judged from the things which were written in the books, according to their deeds. And the sea gave up the dead which were in it, and death and Hades gave up the dead which were in them; and they were judged, every one of them according to their deeds. Then death

*and Hades were thrown into the lake of fire. This is the second
death, the lake of fire. And if anyone's name was not found written in the book of life, he was thrown into the lake of fire.*
—Rev. 20:11-15

Millions of people die every year and tens of thousands every single day. There are more than six billion people in the world, and they
will all die sooner or later; the world's birthrate is more than keeping
up with the death rate. So not only is every person in the world in the
process of dying, but more people are being born to die all the time.
And the sad reality is that all will die in their sins unless they repent
and believe the Gospel. Hell is waiting for its victims.

Clergyman Henry Van Dyke once wrote, "Remember that what
you possess in this world will be found at the day of your death and
belong to someone else; what you are will be yours forever." We can
certainly apply that to someone's spiritual status at the time of his
death and assert that if he or she remains in sin, it will damn them to
hell. Charles Spurgeon expressed the matter much more graphically:
"Many of you are hanging over the mouth of hell by a solitary plank
and that plank is rotten." Thus we see the final and most deadly result
of sin's evil—eternal damnation.

Having looked briefly at sin's definition, its main characteristics,
its universal extent, and its negative results, there remains a conclud-
ing question we must ask of those still trapped in their sins: What can
you do about your sin? The answer is found in Romans 6:23: "For
the wages of sin is death, but the free gift of God is eternal life in
Christ Jesus our Lord."

The apostle Paul expresses two absolute truths in that verse. First,
he reminds us again that spiritual death results from sin. It is the
rightful destiny of every life that is lived apart from God. Second, the
verse tells in one concise statement the remedy for sin's effects—salvation freely granted through Jesus Christ (cf. Eph. 2:8-9). If someone wants what he deserves—eternal death—God will pay him those
wages. But if someone wants what he has heard in the Gospel—eternal life—God will freely grant it, based on faith in Christ's atoning

work. When God's Son died on the cross, He paid the penalty for sin. Now He offers forgiveness for sin to all who believe.

The only genuine happiness we can offer to any sinner is the happiness he can know if his sins are forgiven: "'Blessed are those whose lawless deeds have been forgiven, and whose sins have been covered. Blessed is the man whose sin the Lord will not take into account'" (Rom. 4:7-8; cf. Ps. 32:1-2). That is the *only* remedy for sin and the *true* source of spiritual blessedness that we must proclaim and defend before a lost world.

Chapter 8

THE VIRGIN BIRTH AND DEITY OF JESUS CHRIST

The twentieth century has produced some truly amazing births. The most memorable involved record-setting multiple births, such as the Dionne quintuplets in Canada in the 1930s, the Fischer quintuplets in South Dakota in the 1960s, the Dilley sextuplets in the 1990s, and the McCaughey septuplets in Iowa in 1997. The McCaugheys had seven children thanks to modern fertility drugs, but that fact did not diminish the extraordinary newsworthiness of those births. And we were again astounded in 1998 when a woman in Texas gave birth to eight children, even though she too underwent fertility treatments.

Then there was the truly remarkable single birth in England of Louise Brown—the first "test tube baby"—in the summer of 1978. That was the first time God permitted a baby to be born that had been conceived outside the mother's womb. After more than a decade of specific research, scientists and doctors were able to remove a mother's egg, fertilize it in a lab with sperm taken from the father, place the fertilized egg back into the mother's womb, and let it develop into a child during a normal gestation period. That was amazing news a generation ago, but it has become somewhat common today.

If you want to learn of genuinely miraculous births, however, you must turn to biblical history. Isaac, a patriarch of Israel's redemptive community, was born to Abraham and Sarah when both were over ninety, well past normal child-producing years (cf. Gen. 18:9-14; 21:1-2).

The supernaturally empowered Samson was born to Manoah and his barren wife, just as the angel of the Lord said (Judges 13:2-5,

24). Though born naturally he was enabled by God to perform great feats of courage and strength as one of the last judges of Israel.

Then Samuel, judge, prophet, priest, and anointer of kings, was born to the previously barren Hannah. His birth was the direct result of his humble and godly mother's prayers and the intervention of the Lord (1 Sam. 1:11, 19-20).

Finally, in the New Testament, John the Baptist was born to Zacharias and barren Elizabeth, a couple between sixty and eighty who had never been able to have children (Luke 1:5-17). John, whom Jesus called the greatest man ever born, was filled with the Holy Spirit and was the forerunner of the Messiah.

So history reports a number of astounding natural births. Some of those in our day were aided by scientific advances, whereas those referred to from Bible times resulted from God's supernatural intervention. While the events surrounding those births were truly amazing, none of them compares with the virgin birth of the God/man Jesus Christ. They cannot equal the divine display in His conception and birth.

THE FOUNDATION OF CHRIST'S DEITY: HIS VIRGIN BIRTH

During more than thirty years of preaching and teaching the Bible, people have periodically asked me this question: To be truly saved, is it essential for someone to believe that Jesus was conceived by the Holy Spirit in a virgin? I've always told them it is. To be saved you must believe in the true Christ, the God/man, and that truth originates in the doctrine of the virgin conception and birth. This is a truth you and I must stand for as we proclaim the Gospel to the lost.

The virgin conception and birth of the Lord Jesus Christ is a unique event, and it is absolutely critical to Christian theology, which says the Savior is both Son of God and Son of Man. He had to be born of God to be divine, and born of a woman (Mary) to be human, so that since the founding of the church, the virgin conception has been upheld as an essential doctrine. Here's what respected theologian and Bible commentator F. F. Bruce wrote:

The church's confession, as we trace it back to primitive times, sets alongside the fact of our Lord's incarnation the claim that He became incarnate through being conceived by the power of the Holy Spirit in the womb of the Virgin Mary.

There are those, indeed, who acknowledge our Lord's incarnation without believing in His virgin birth, just as others, Muslims for example, believe in His virgin birth but not in His incarnation. But it is undeniable that His incarnation and virgin birth are intimately bound together in the historic faith of the church. Nor is this surprising. The incarnation was a supernatural event—an unprecedented and unrepeated act of God. The more we appreciate the uniqueness of the incarnation, the more may we recognize how fitting—indeed, how inevitable—it is that the means by which it was brought about should also be unique. Our Lord's virginal conception must certainly be understood as a pure miracle; attempts to explain it by analogies . . . are worse than useless. ("The Person of Christ: Incarnation and Virgin Birth," in *Basic Christian Doctrines*, ed. Carl F. H. Henry [Grand Rapids, Mich.: Baker, 1971 reprint], 128)

In his well-known account of Jesus' birth in the Gospel of Luke, the evangelist wanted us to understand the importance of this miracle. As astonishing, humanly inexplicable, and beyond scientific explanation as it was, we are nevertheless called in the simplest terms to accept the miracle of the virgin conception of Christ in Mary's womb as a reality. Here's Luke's straightforward account of the first news to the virgin Mary that God would place His Son Jesus in her womb, without participation by a man:

And the angel said to her, "Do not be afraid, Mary; for you have found favor with God. And behold, you will conceive in your womb and bear a son, and you shall name Him Jesus. He will be great, and will be called the Son of the Most High; and the Lord God will give Him the throne of His father David; and He will reign over the house of Jacob forever; and His kingdom will have

no end." And Mary said to the angel, "How can this be, since I
am a virgin?" The angel answered and said to her, "The Holy
Spirit will come upon you, and the power of the Most High will
overshadow you; and for that reason the holy offspring shall be
called the Son of God."

—*Luke 1:30-35*

The angel Gabriel's announcement to Mary derived from several important foundations. The announcement to Mary was not some novel, fanciful invention, but it was based on solid historical and doctrinal foundations.

The Foundation of the Old Testament

The first foundation for the reality of the virgin conception is Old Testament prophecy. As early as Genesis 3:15 Christ's supernatural birth was clearly implied: "And I will put enmity between you and the woman, and between your seed and her seed; he shall bruise you on the head, and you shall bruise him on the heel." That was part of God's judgment on Satan following the Fall, and it was the first prophecy that looked forward to redemption. The one called "her seed," who would deal a crushing blow to Satan's head, could be none other than Christ. Satan would bruise His heel at the crucifixion, but Christ would rise from the grave and give the fatal blow to Satan's head (to be ultimately executed when the devil will be sentenced and cast into the Lake of Fire forever).

The expression "her seed" also must refer to someone other than Mary because women do not naturally produce seed. However, it is natural for the man to have seed (cf. Gen. 12:1-3; Gal. 3:16). How could a woman have a seed? Only by the one-time-only, supernatural intervention of the Holy Spirit to place the divine seed into the womb of Mary—an unmistakable allusion to Jesus Christ's virgin conception.

Psalm 2:7-9 provides another foundation for the virgin birth and deity of Christ: "I will surely tell of the decree of the LORD: He said to Me, 'Thou art My Son, today I have begotten Thee. Ask of Me, and I will surely give the nations as Thine inheritance, and the very ends of the earth as Thy possession. Thou shalt break them with a rod of iron, Thou shalt shatter them like earthenware.'" This is the only Old Testament reference to the relationship between the Father and the Son, one that was sovereignly planned in eternity past and fulfilled in Christ's incarnation. The passage is also a Messianic prophecy (cf. vv. 8-9) that promised God would bring One into the world to rule it with "a rod of iron," who would be His Son.

If the unbelieving Jews of Jesus' day had properly understood Psalm 2, they would have realized that Christ had to be as the angel Gabriel had said, "Son of the Most High" God, as well as a human ancestor of David through Mary (as His geneaology in Luke 3 shows). Anyone who carefully considers Scripture's claims would have seen that the virgin birth was very central to Messiah's coming.

Isaiah 7:14 is another key Old Testament passage that validates the truth of the virgin pregnancy. With words now so familiar to us, the prophet Isaiah declared the clear prophetic sign of how God would work to bring about the incarnation: "Therefore the LORD Himself will give you a sign: Behold, a virgin will be with child and bear a son, and she will call His name Immanuel."

The English word "virgin" in this context is the correct rendering of the Hebrew *almah*. The word denotes a woman who is truly a virgin, not merely a young or unmarried woman. This translation is consistent with the meaning of the word in seven of eight other Old Testament occurrences.

The correct intent of Isaiah's prophecy is strongly corroborated by Matthew's inspired interpretation of it: "'She [Mary] will bear a Son; and you [Joseph] shall call His name Jesus, for it is He who will save His people from their sins.' Now all this took place that what was spoken by the Lord through the prophet might be fulfilled: 'Behold, the virgin shall be with child, and shall bear a Son, and they shall call His name Immanuel,' which translated means, 'God with us'" (Matt. 1:21-23).

Matthew used *parthenos* for "virgin," which is the Greek equivalent of *almah*. Whenever a form of *parthenos* is used in the New

Testament (including in Luke), it always means virgin, one who has had no sexual relations at all. This fact further underscores that Matthew correctly understood Isaiah's usage of the term and the prophet's genuine intention to predict that Messiah would be born of a virgin. Matthew's interpretation is also hard to dispute because he simply reported the message from the angel of the Lord (Matt. 1:20), a perfectly trustworthy messenger.

So Mary the mother of Jesus was truly a virgin, in accord with the sign predicted in Isaiah 7:14. If a woman became pregnant and had a son, that was not a special sign; it was a normal occurrence. But if a virgin became pregnant and brought a son into the world—and one of his names was "God with us"—that was unmistakably a miraculous divine sign.

The Foundation of Messiah's Person and Work

The role of Messiah, foreseen by the Old Testament prophets and confirmed by the New Testament, provides a second major foundation for the reality of Jesus Christ's virgin birth. If the Scripture verses we are about to look at have a valid interrelationship—and they do—then we can make the reasonable conclusion that Jesus had to be the Son of God. And in order to be God's Son and our Savior, He had to be placed by God in the womb of a virgin.

The prophet Isaiah quotes God this way: "I, even I, am the LORD; and there is no savior besides Me. . . . Turn to Me, and be saved, all the ends of the earth; for I am God, and there is no other" (Isa. 43:11; 45:22). In the New Testament, the apostle Paul tells Timothy and Titus four times that God is the Savior (1 Tim. 2:3-4; Titus 2:10, 13; 3:4). Earlier the Gospel writers had already identified Jesus as the Savior: "You shall call His name Jesus, for it is He who will save His people from their sins" (Matt. 1:21; cf. Luke 2:11). Therefore we can stand confidently on the truth of this logic: God is the only Savior; Jesus is a Savior; therefore Jesus is God (cf. Acts 4:12).

The Old Testament, through the prophets, also identifies God as our only Redeemer: "Thus says the Lord your Redeemer, the Holy

One of Israel" (Isa. 43:14; cf. Hos. 13:14). This truth is again supported by the New Testament: "Blessed be the Lord God of Israel, for He has visited us and accomplished redemption for His people" (Luke 1:68); "Christ redeemed us from the curse of the Law" (Gal. 3:13); "You were not redeemed with perishable things like silver or gold from your futile way of life inherited from your forefathers, but with precious blood, as of a lamb unblemished and spotless, the blood of Christ" (1 Pet. 1:18-19).

The relationship and logical sequence of those Scriptures lead to just one valid conclusion: If God is the only Redeemer, and Christ redeemed us, then Christ is God. And since Christ is God and the preexisting second member of the Trinity, the incarnation had to be by means of a miraculous coming together of the divine and the human—namely, the virgin conception and birth.

All of those truths about the Person and work of Christ bring us to one ultimate truth about Him, contained in both Testaments: He alone is worthy of worship. Moses reiterated to the Israelites this command from the Ten Commandments: "You shall fear only the LORD your God; and you shall worship Him, and swear by His name" (Deut. 6:13). Then centuries later the writer of the letter to the Hebrews told his believing Jewish audience, "And when He again brings the first-born [Christ] into the world, He says, 'And let all the angels of God worship Him'" (Heb. 1:6). If God Himself calls angels and people to worship Christ, and if worship is reserved only for God, then Christ is God (cf. Isa. 45:23; Phil. 2:9-11).

So the scriptural foundations for the reality of Christ's virgin birth are firmly established. You can lead any doubting unbeliever to them if necessary. For one thing, they clearly refute the notion that the doctrine of the virgin birth is merely a man-made invention to somehow elevate Jesus to a mystical position above the average person. Nothing could be further from the truth. The Old Testament said Christ would be the Son of God and born of a virgin, and the very Person and work of Christ as Savior demanded that His incarnation come by the Holy Spirit through a virgin. The New Testament recorded the fulfillment of it all, most thoroughly in Luke 1, where the evangelist presents the announcement of our Savior's miraculous birth to the virgin Mary.

THE MIRACLE OF THE VIRGIN BIRTH

Two thousand years ago God entered this world as a human being. On that well-known night, a baby boy was born who was unlike any other before or since—the God/man, Jesus Christ. His birth was so monumental that it became the demarcation point of history. Everything that happened before this event was identified as B.C. (commonly understood as *before Christ*), everything after as A.D. (*anno Domini*, Latin for "the year of our Lord").

Luke, the careful historian and theologian, reported Mary's response to the announcement of Christ's conception and virgin birth concisely but with sufficient detail:

> And Mary said to the angel, "How can this be, since I am a virgin?" The angel answered and said to her, "The Holy Spirit will come upon you, and the power of the Most High will overshadow you; and for that reason the holy offspring shall be called the Son of God. And behold, even your relative Elizabeth has also conceived a son in her old age; and she who was called barren is now in her sixth month. For nothing will be impossible with God." And Mary said, "Behold, the bondslave of the Lord; may it be done to me according to your word." And the angel departed from her.
>
> —Luke 1:34-38

The truth of this narrative unfolds from five basic facts: Mary's question to the angel, God's omnipotent strategy, God's sign to Mary, God's sovereignty in the miracle, and Mary's submission to God's will.

Mary's Question to the Angel

The young teenager Mary (probably about thirteen years old) was shaken to the core of her being over this encounter with a divine messenger. Luke 1:29-30 indicates that she was fearfully pondering the angel's initial words and had to be encouraged by him not to be frightened.

In response to the astonishing truth just given to her that she would be the mother of the Son of God (vv. 31-33), Mary asked the basic question as to the means. "How can this be, since I am a virgin?" is not a question of doubt or unbelief. Mary did believe the angel's words from God; she simply wanted to know how such an impossible thing would be fulfilled.

A big reason Mary sought clarification of the angel's words was that she was not accustomed to dealing with supernatural appearances and miraculous promises. No one in her day was. There had been no divine revelation in more than 400 years, since the completion of the Old Testament. And no series of miraculous events had occurred since the days of Elijah, nearly a half a millenium earlier.

Mary believed Gabriel's promise, as anyone who loved God would. She was honestly perplexed and overwhelmed by what, in all human life, was an extraordinary and unprecedented event. But her question also indicated that she *did* understand what the angel was *not* saying to her.

Mary realized the angel was not saying she was merely going to marry Joseph and have a child by him. There would be nothing miraculous in that. Instead, her testimony to her virginity ("since I am a virgin") reveals she knew she would conceive a son right away, before she married anyone. Mary understood what was about to happen, but she couldn't help wondering how God would do it.

God's Omnipotent Strategy

The angel Gabriel answered Mary's question by revealing God's omnipotent and amazing strategy: the Holy Spirit would come upon her (v. 35). The Spirit of God, who was the original agent of creation (Gen. 1:2), would again become an agent of God's special creation, this time in the womb of a teenaged girl. There is no suggestion in Luke 1 or any other Scripture text that human sexual activity produced Mary's child, Jesus. God's Word indicates that only divine, creative power acted on Mary, which validates again the truth of the virgin birth.

The angel then enhanced Mary's understanding by asserting, "the power of the Most High will overshadow you." "Most High" is simply another title for the Holy Spirit and is from the Hebrew *El Elyon*, "God Most High." It is a very common Old Testament name for God and means "almighty, all-powerful, sovereign ruler." It denotes One who is sovereign over everything in heaven and on earth—the Creator God who made and upholds the universe and who initiated Jesus' virgin conception and birth.

God Himself would surround and influence ("overshadow") Mary's womb with creative power to produce a special child. Because of that creative miracle, "the holy offspring shall be called the Son of God." That statement amplifies further our understanding of the virgin birth and the deity of Christ in two significant ways.

First, Mary's son would be unlike any other person ever born because God would create Him "holy" (separate from any sin). Second, because God Himself would create Mary's child in her womb, that "holy offspring" would be truly, by nature, the Son of God, not the son of Mary and Joseph. Jesus would be God in human flesh (cf. Ps. 2:7; John 1:1-2, 14; Heb. 1:3).

God's Sign to Mary

The angel's news about the unique and extraordinary birth was so mind-boggling to Mary that God graciously gave her a sign to further confirm the truth of all He was saying through the angel. Mary had responded in humble faith, without demanding a sign; but God in His sovereign wisdom gave her one that would strengthen her faith.

The sign God chose for Mary was the miraculous pregnancy of her older relative, Elizabeth: "And behold, even your relative Elizabeth has also conceived a son in her old age; and she who was called barren is now in her sixth month" (Luke 1:36).

Even though she was a young teenager, Mary was aware that Elizabeth, in her sixties or seventies, had been unable to have any children all those years. So the news that her elderly relative was then in her sixth month of pregnancy was quite startling for Mary.

The miracle of Elizabeth's pregnancy was also a conception miracle, but not in the same way that Mary's would be. Unlike the virgin conception that was to occur in Mary's womb, Elizabeth conceived a son in the normal fashion with her husband, but with miraculous help from God to overrule her lifelong barrenness. He graciously intervened in the life of an older couple to allow them to conceive.

God's amazing work on Elizabeth's behalf was a wonderful, affirming sign that conception miracles were possible. Mary could by visiting Elizabeth see firsthand the miracle of conception because of God's miraculous intervention (cf. Luke 1:39-40).

God's Sovereignty in the Miracle

No matter how humanly impossible, God is able to fulfill everything He promises, and He reminded Mary of that fact with a short but profound statement about His omnipotence: "For nothing will be impossible with God" (Luke 1:37).

That truth, again delivered by the angel Gabriel, first accompanied the promise of another miracle—Isaac's birth to Abraham and Sarah (Gen. 18:10-14). They were even further beyond their childbearing years than Zacharias and Elizabeth, but God assured Abraham and Sarah that they would have a special son. At first Sarah laughed in unbelief at God's promise (vv. 12-13, 15). That prompted Him to ask Abraham, "Is anything too difficult for the LORD?" (v. 14), which was the basis of Gabriel's words to Mary.

As a God-fearing Jew, Mary was undoubtedly aware of the Old Testament assertions regarding divine sovereignty (e.g., Ps. 115:3; Jer. 32:17; Dan. 4:35). But the specific allusion to Genesis 18:14 reminded her that in the past nothing was impossible concerning the conception of a child. Undoubtedly, thoughts such as *What's going on here?* and *This is impossible!* continued to swirl in Mary's mind. Therefore she needed additional reminders, as all of us often do, that God's limitless power can accomplish whatever He pleases. If nothing was too difficult for Him in the past (the miraculous birth of Isaac, the divinely assisted conception of John the Baptist), then everything is possible in the future with Him (including the virgin conception of Christ).

Mary's Submission to God's Will

After the angel answered Mary's question and she heard how God could and would make her the virgin mother of His Son, she responded in the way most fitting for a servant of the Lord—she humbly submitted to His will.

When Mary responded with the words, "Behold, the bondslave of the Lord; may it be done to me according to your word" (Luke 1:38), she demonstrated knowledge of another important Old Testament story of a miracle birth—the account of how God answered Hannah's prayer by enabling her to have the special child Samuel (1 Sam. 1—2).

Mary followed Hannah's example of being a willing bondslave and obediently bowed to the incredible unfolding of God's purposes. Hannah referred to herself four times as a "maidservant" (1 Sam. 1:11, 18), which in the Greek Old Testament (LXX) is the same word (doule) that Mary used in Luke to call herself a "bondslave." Mary was apparently familiar with God's miracle that allowed Hannah, a woman who had long been childless, to conceive and bear Samuel. Thus the young virgin chosen by God to conceive and bear the Messiah also saw herself as a humble servant committed to God's sovereign purpose (cf. Luke 1:48).

Mary's final words to the angel in Luke 1:38, "may it be done to me according to your word," indicate that she understood and accepted by faith the implications of all that Gabriel said was soon to happen to her. She surely realized how impossible it would be for her to convince people that she, a thirteen-year-old girl, was pregnant by the Holy Spirit! Even Joseph would find that impossible to swallow and would be certain she had sinned. And Joseph was indeed trying to decide whether she should be stoned for her sin, or whether he should end the betrothal, until he received a message from the Lord recorded in Mathew 1:20-25, especially verse 20: "Do not be afraid to take Mary as your wife; for that which has been conceived in her is of the Holy Spirit." Instead of worrying about what the outcome would be when Joseph and others realized her condition, Mary as a submissive servant left all the details to God and rested in His purposes.

The announcement about the virgin birth in the Gospel of Luke is an astonishing account. The narrative contains simple, brief verses with no unnecessary details. At the same time, Luke, historian and evangelist, retained in it elements of profound theological truth veiled in mystery. Neither he nor any of the other Gospel writers provide an in-depth explanation of how the virgin conception and birth occurred. But in God's foreordained plan our Lord and Savior Jesus Christ *was* born to a virgin. That fundamental truth was not dependent on elaborate, detailed commentary, even from Spirit-inspired writers of Scripture. The virgin birth is a doctrine that is not fully describable to the human mind, but it is an essential one to preserve the nature of Jesus as the Savior who was God and man.

So the virgin conception and deity of Christ are essential to the Christian message and are critical to explain and defend as you and I share the Gospel with the lost.

Chapter 9

THE DEATH AND RESURRECTION OF JESUS CHRIST

The death and resurrection of Jesus Christ are the culmination of redemptive history, the primary events of God's plan of salvation. Yet over the centuries these two great truths of history have been respectively misunderstood and factually rejected. The significance of Christ's death has been erroneously interpreted as simply the execution of a social revolutionary, the unjust martyrdom of a noble idealist, or the dramatic conclusion to an interesting but ofttimes puzzling interlude in Middle Eastern religious history. And rationalists and skeptics have dismissed the Resurrection as an impossibility or as a hoax or fabrication propagated by the disciples as part of the dogma of a new religion.

The majority of people in contemporary society have been heavily influenced by those viewpoints concerning our Lord's atoning death and supernatural, bodily resurrection. They have no practical grasp of what God's Word teaches about those momentous events, nor of the spiritual, life-changing application He desires those facts to have in the lives of every individual. That's why no study of the basic truths we believe and proclaim is complete without a scriptural examination of Christ's crucifixion and resurrection.

THE CRUCIFIXION: A BACKDROP

It is quite probable that some of the more than 30,000 men crucified in the Holy Land around the time of Christ were innocent victims.

Most of them, however, were fanatical patriots who hoped to free the Jews and others from the oppression of Rome. They were executed for sedition and armed insurrection, and the majority were probably admired as people who died for a cause they truly believed in. But why does history remember the name of only one man who was crucified during those tumultuous times—Jesus Christ? And why does the Bible record so much about the details and significance of His death?

The answers to those questions begin to emerge in the early chapters of Scripture. First, the sin of Adam and Eve in Genesis 3 caused them and all their descendants to fall under the curse and corruption of sin. But immediately after the Fall, God already gave mankind hope for deliverance. In Genesis 3:15 He delivered the first promise of the Gospel when He said to Satan: "I will put enmity between you and the woman, and between your seed and her seed [Christ]; he shall bruise you on the head, and you shall bruise him on the heel." Satan would temporarily bruise Christ's heel through the crucifixion, but Christ would bruise Satan permanently "on the head" with His victory over sin and death through the Resurrection.

Second, the Old Testament sacrificial system, previewed in the first Passover (Exodus 12) and fully prescribed in Leviticus, told God's people that blood had to be shed for the remission of sin. But those animal sacrifices, repeated continually during Israel's history, simply *pictured* the real, once-for-all, sufficient sacrifice of Jesus' death on the cross. The animals' blood had no power to permanently cleanse people from sin; only Christ's blood shed at Calvary could do that (Heb. 10:4; 1 John 1:7).

Third, the prophets foresaw that the coming Messiah's earthly mission would be to die for the sins of His people. Isaiah said, "As a result of the anguish of His soul, He will see it and be satisfied; by His knowledge the Righteous One, My Servant, will justify the many, as He will bear their iniquities" (Isa. 53:11; cf. the full context, 52:13—53:10). Zechariah wrote of the Jews, "they will look on Me whom they have pierced; and they will mourn for Him, as one mourns for an only son" (Zech. 12:10). The prophet knew that one day God's chosen people would turn to the Christ whom they crucified.

Finally, the apostles clearly explained and emphasized the importance of Jesus' death. Paul said that at Calvary Christ became a curse for us who deserved to be cursed (Gal. 3:13). First Peter 3:18 concludes that our Lord "died for sins once for all, the just for the unjust, so that He might bring us to God, having been put to death in the flesh, but made alive in the spirit" (cf. Heb. 9:28). And finally the apostle John, in the last book of the New Testament, called Jesus the ultimate sacrifice: "Thou wast slain, and didst purchase for God with Thy blood men from every tribe and tongue and people and nation" (Rev. 5:9; cf. 13:8).

Therefore, the essence of what we must proclaim in the Gospel is the death of Jesus Christ. That was the supreme revelation of God's gracious love for a sinful world and the basis of forgiveness. As witnesses for Him and the message of salvation, we need a basic understanding of what happened that day on the cross and of those events' continuing relevance for sinners today.

THE MIRACLES OF THE CROSS

All four Gospels contain accurate narratives of Christ's death, but I believe none of them delineates its meaning as effectively as Matthew 27:45-53. There the apostle Matthew reports six miracles that accompanied the crucifixion: the supernatural darkness, Christ's separation from His Father, Christ's self-giving death, the divine tearing of the temple veil, the supernatural earthquake, and the supernatural opening of many tombs. Those amazing events give us a useful and unequaled divine commentary on the meaning of our Savior's death.

God Sends Darkness

The first miracle during the crucifixion was a period of darkness that fell over the land from noon until 3:00 P.M. Jesus' executioners nailed Him to the cross at about 9:00 A.M. (Mark 15:25); so when the darkness started, He had already been on the cross for three hours.

Those first three hours of crucifixion were essentially a period of silence, interrupted only by Jesus' words of gracious forgiveness and kindness toward various people (His enemies, Luke 23:34; the penitent thief, v. 43; and His mother, John 19:26-27).

The supernatural darkness that marked His second three hours on the cross may have been local or universal. Matthew 27:45 reports it this way: "Now from the sixth hour darkness fell upon all the land until the ninth hour." We can also translate the Greek word for "land" with the English word *earth*, which means the entire world. Therefore this text does not indicate precisely how widespread the darkness was. Of course, God's omnipotence could have made it either local or universal (cf. Exod. 10:14-15; Josh. 10:12-13; 2 Kings 20:9-11).

Whatever its extent, the darkness was a miraculous occurrence. In his Gospel, Luke used the Greek word *ekleipo* to describe what happened. That is the word from which we get the English word *eclipse*, and it literally means to fail or cease to exist. But a natural solar eclipse does not explain the darkness, because ancient calendars indicate that the sun and moon were too far apart that day. Luke implicitly recognized that God had intervened, and thus he simply wrote, "the sun being obscured" (Luke 23:45).

The Bible does not explain the purpose for this extraordinary darkness. But consistent with other descriptive uses of that term in Scripture, the crucifixion darkness was most likely a sign of God's judgment against the heinous sin of killing His Son. The prophets used words for darkness in describing the Day of the Lord (e.g., Isa. 13:10-11; Joel 2:2; Zeph. 1:14-15). The New Testament writers also associated darkness with God's judgment (e.g., Matt. 8:12; 22:13; 25:30; 2 Pet. 2:4; Jude 6).

The cross of Jesus was definitely a place of judgment. There God placed our sins on the shoulders of His own sinless, perfect Son. Supernatural darkness was therefore an appropriate reaction to display God's intense displeasure with sin poured out on His Son, the innocent substitute.

God Sovereignly Departs from His Son

At the end of the period of darkness, a second, even more inexplicable event occurred when God the Father temporarily separated Himself from Christ the Son. Jesus expressed His anguish because of this, as reported by Matthew: "And about the ninth hour Jesus cried out with a loud voice, saying, 'Eli, Eli, lama sabachthani?' that is, 'My God, My God, why hast Thou forsaken Me?'" (27:46).

Jesus was crying out in distress because that separation from God was the first and only such experience He would ever have. His Father was temporarily turning His back on Him because the Son had become sin in the place of sinners. Somehow, in the profound mystery of God's sovereignty and omnipotence, the Father removed Himself briefly from normal fellowship with Christ. God forsook Christ and poured out His wrath on the sinless Savior because He "who knew no sin [became] sin on our behalf" (2 Cor. 5:21). Jesus also became "a curse for us" (Gal. 3:13) and was "the propitiation for our sins" (1 John 4:10; cf. Isa. 53:5; Rom. 4:25; 1 Cor. 15:3; 1 Pet. 2:24; 3:18).

Our Lord Jesus *bore* our sin in the sense that He was punished for it all, so that those who trust in His work of redemption would be rescued from the penalty of their sin.

God's departure from His only begotten Son was not a separation of essence or substance. Jesus did not suddenly cease to be the Son of God and the second Person of the Trinity any more than a child who is being punished by his human father ceases being that father's son or daughter. However, Christ did for a short but intense period of time cease to experience intimate fellowship with His heavenly Father, analogous to a disobedient child's temporarily ceasing to have his normal, loving fellowship with an earthly father.

The mystery of Christ's separation from God is too profound for any of us to grasp completely. But you and I can see the reality of Christ's substitutionary death and appreciate something of the pain of His separation from God when we contemplate the crucifixion.

We need to convey the truth of this reality to others as we share the Gospel with them. We can say that Jesus willingly suffered for sinners, and that He writhed in agony under the judgment of God for sins He did not and could not commit, and in that experience, He endured the extremely painful loss of fellowship with His Father.

Christ Gives Up His Own Life

The Lord's willingness and ability to control the giving up of His life was the third miracle of the cross (Matt. 27:50; Luke 23:46). This was Jesus' willing sacrifice for sin, in accordance with God's redemptive plan. Unlike others who were crucified, He did not gradually fade away and die many hours later from suffocation. Instead, as Matthew reports, Christ "yielded up His spirit" (27:50). The Greek word translated "yielded up" means to let go or send away by an act of the will. Thus Jesus' executioners did not take His life; He voluntarily surrendered it by an act of His sovereign will.

This third miracle of the cross exactly fulfilled the Lord's earlier statement to the disciples: "No one has taken it [My life] away from Me, but I lay it down on My own initiative. I have authority to lay it down, and I have authority to take it up again" (John 10:18).

Jesus had just shouted those profound words, "It is finished!" (John 19:30), indicating He had completed the work of redemption. That He even had the strength to cry out in a loud voice at this point was itself amazing. He had a reserve of energy unheard of for someone with such severe bodily injuries. Though Christ should have been much weaker, He also should have taken longer to die. His early death on the cross surprised Pontius Pilate, the Roman governor, who had to ask a centurion for verification (Mark 15:43-45).

Everything surrounding this third miracle of the cross underscores that the Son of God divinely controls living and dying. He did not take His own life, nor was He helplessly at the mercy of His enemies' plan to kill Him. Instead, Christ willingly and in obedience to God's plan surrendered His life as a sacrifice to pay the penalty for man's sin.

God Tears the Temple Veil

Right after Jesus gave up His life, a fourth miracle of great significance occurred: "the veil of the temple was torn in two from top to bottom" (Matt. 27:51a).

The veil was a massive, predominantly blue curtain that separated the Holy of Holies ("temple"), where God symbolically dwelt, from the rest of the temple area. Every year on the Day of Atonement the Jewish high priest went through the veil to sprinkle blood on the altar for the people's sins. That symbolic ritual had to be repeated every year in anticipation of the true, once-for-all sacrifice for sin that Messiah would someday offer.

When Christ breathed His last breath on the cross, the final sacrifice for sin was completed, and the veil separating the Holy of Holies was no longer needed. This dramatically symbolized that God was accessible to all at all times, not just the High Priest once a year—men and women could now come directly to God through Christ without the help of priests or repeated ritual sacrifices. Consequently, God's miraculous tearing of the temple veil from the top down signified that the barrier of sin was forever removed for all who believe in Christ's saving work and want to draw near to God (cf. Heb. 4:16). What an encouraging and vital truth to share with those to whom we are witnessing. God is available to the sinner.

God Causes an Earthquake

When Jesus yielded up His life and the temple veil parted, "the earth shook; and the rocks were split" (Matt. 27:51)—a fifth miracle associated with Jesus' crucifixion. It was another clear sign from God about the importance of His Son's death.

God sometimes used earthquakes in the Old Testament to underscore the importance of special events. At Mt. Sinai "the whole mountain quaked violently" (Exod. 19:18). When God appeared to Elijah on a mountain, "A great and strong wind was rending the mountains and breaking in pieces the rocks before the LORD. . . . And after the wind an earthquake" (1 Kings 19:11).

In the New Testament, writers employed similar imagery. In Revelation 6:12 the apostle John said, "I looked when He broke the sixth seal, and there was a great earthquake" (cf. Heb. 12:26-27).

When Jesus died on the cross, God ratified the Son's possession of the title deed to the earth (cf. Phil. 2:8-11; Rev. 5:9-10). The supernatural earthquake was therefore a preview of what God will do on a greater scale prior to the final return of His Son: "And there were flashes of lightning and sounds and peals of thunder; and there was a great earthquake, such as there had not been since man came to be upon the earth, so great an earthquake was it, and so mighty" (Rev. 16:18; cf. 6:12; 8:5; 11:13). God had the right to declare that Jesus indeed was King of kings and Lord of lords.

God Opens Many Tombs

Just as the miraculous earthquake at Christ's death indicated in advance some events of the end-times, so did the sixth supernatural event—the opening of graves and the raising to life of many believers.

Any strong earthquake could break open tombs. However, the amazing final miracle was that "many bodies of the saints who had fallen asleep were raised" (Matt. 27:52). Matthew's description makes it clear, however, that not all believers were raised in that miracle. God sovereignly selected "many" but not all believers to be raised from the dead. For them it was their final resurrection and glorification, just as eventually it will be for all believers (1 Thess. 4:16).

Those who arose right after the earthquake did not appear in Jerusalem until after Christ's own resurrection (Matt. 27:53), because as the risen Savior He was "the first fruits of those who are asleep" (1 Cor. 15:20). When they did appear to others (likely other believers), they probably did so just long enough to verify the reality of this last miracle of Jesus' death. Then they likely ascended to heaven, which is why nothing more is said in Scripture about them.

In pointing to the preceding six miracles of Christ's death, we can assure anyone who is spiritually lost that the amazing display of supernatural power takes that event out of any human category and makes the cross the true and only hope of eternal life. When Christ died, God's wrath against sin (depicted by the darkness and sovereign separation) was appeased. Christ's death was a voluntary one, so that all who trust in Him will have open access to God (through the veil) and a true hope of future resurrection and glorification. In those ways God emphasized for all time the significance of His Son's death on a cross. However, that death was by no means the end of the story.

THE IMPORTANCE OF THE RESURRECTION

The greatest distinction between Christianity and other religions is that the death of its founder did not mark the termination of His life and ministry. For Christians, the death of Jesus Christ did not mean His deteriorating remains had to be placed in a permanent tomb outside Jerusalem, Bethlehem, or anywhere else. A follower of Buddha, on the other hand, once wrote, "When Buddha died it was with that utter passing away in which nothing whatever remains." And Mohammed, the founder of Islam, died in A.D. 632 and was buried. Since then, tens of thousands of Muslims have annually visited his tomb in Medina, Saudi Arabia—not to celebrate his resurrection, but to mourn his death. However, you and I celebrate every Lord's Day, and especially on Easter Sunday and in services of immersion baptism, the victory of our Lord Jesus over death and the grave.

The Resurrection is the hinge on which the truth of our faith turns, and without it nothing else would really matter. Without the historical fact of Jesus' resurrection, the significance of the crucifixion would be nullified, and all the other doctrines we proclaim and defend to the world would be just so much rhetoric. The dynamic joy of our faith would turn into speculation, and Christianity would be simply one of many human philosophies and religious theories.

Every truth our Lord taught during His earthly ministry revolved around His upcoming resurrection. This is what He promised to His disciples and friends: "The Son of Man must suffer many things and be rejected by the elders and the chief priests and the scribes, and be killed, and after three days rise again" (Mark 8:31; cf. 9:9, 31); "I am the resurrection and the life; he who believes in Me shall live even if he dies" (John 11:25). The disciples also carried forth that theme, as demonstrated by Peter's first two sermons (Acts 2:14-36; 3:12-26).

A conviction that the Resurrection was true transformed the fearful, grieving disciples into courageous evangelists and martyrs who carried the gospel message to all the known world. People in the early church knew that, like Christ, they would one day rise to new life and dwell forever with Him in heaven. That motivated them to face ridicule, prison, torture, and death in order to tell the world about the risen Lord and Savior. Because our hope of glory is the same as the early believers', we should model their attitude as we proclaim Christ to those without hope of eternal life.

Without the resurrection, the life-giving power of the Gospel and the promises of dwelling forever with Christ in heaven are nullified. If Jesus remained in the tomb, those who profess trust in Him cannot hope for a better fate (cf. 1 Cor. 15:19). The doctrine of the resurrection is an essential part of the Gospel; without it salvation can't be provided or received. That's why the apostle Paul told the Romans, "If you confess with your mouth Jesus as Lord, and believe in your heart that God *raised Him from the dead*, you shall be saved" (10:9, emphasis added). It's also why he listed key evidences for the resurrection in one of the most well-known chapters in his New Testament letters.

EVIDENCES FOR THE RESURRECTION

Paul devoted the entire fifteenth chapter of 1 Corinthians to the doctrine of Christ's resurrection and the future resurrection of believers. That he would devote one long section to an explanation of the resurrection indicates something of its importance to us. In the first eleven verses the apostle gives an excellent foundation for the truth of the resurrection. He outlines five basic evidences for this doctrine that we ought to study and grasp: the church's testimony, the Scriptures' testimony, the eyewitnesses' testimony, Paul's own testimony, and the testimony of a common message. (For an in-depth discussion of the entire chapter, see my *1 Corinthians*, MacArthur New Testament Commentary [Chicago: Moody Press, 1984], chaps. 40-45.)

The Church's Testimony

The church's testimony to Christ's resurrection is not explicitly stated but is implied in 1 Corinthians 15:1-2. That the Gospel had miraculously changed the Corinthians when they accepted it in repentance and faith strongly attests to its power, a power sustained by the truth of the resurrection. Even though the church at Corinth was troubled by quarrels and divisions, immorality, incorrect practices in its services, and the presence of some false believers, the living Savior dwelt in and worked through the Corinthian Christians. Paul recognized that divine presence and did not hesitate to again call the recipients of his letter "brethren" (15:1; cf. 1:10; 2:1; 3:1; 10:1) as he began instructing them concerning the resurrection.

The endurance of the Christian church during the 2,000 years since Corinth is further evidence of the truth of the resurrection. The Body of Christ has survived many persecutions, varieties of heresy, much unfaithfulness, and skepticism of all sorts during that period. Critics have dismissed Jesus' resurrection as a myth or a fabrication. However, they have never explained how such a fabrication could motivate Christians to sacrifice everything, even their freedom and lives at certain times, in devotion and loyalty to a dead Lord. A church that is alive and persevering is proof that Christ Himself is alive; and He is alive because God raised Him from the dead.

Church historian Roland H. Bainton wrote this about the importance of Christ's resurrection to the establishment and growth of the early church:

> The resurrection made the Church. Perhaps without it there might have been a church, for Paul tells us that the Lord appeared to 500 brethren at once. They had assembled before their experience of the resurrection. The cross had brought them together, but would they have remained together, would they have established a new religion had

they proclaimed only Christ crucified and not also Christ risen from the dead? (*Early Christianity* [New York: Van Nostrand Reinhold, 1960], 16)

The Scriptures' Testimony

Paul cited a second evidence for the validity of the resurrection: "For I delivered to you as of first importance what I also received, that Christ died for our sins *according to the Scriptures*, and that He was buried, and that He was raised on the third day *according to the Scriptures*" (1 Cor. 15:3-4, emphases added). For the apostle at that time, "the Scriptures" were the Old Testament writings that had clearly foreseen Christ's death, burial, and resurrection. Concerning Scripture's reliability and authority on those subjects, Paul was simply following Jesus' pattern.

When the Savior dealt with the men on the Emmaus road, our Lord pointed them to the sure teachings of the Old Testament: "'O foolish men and slow of heart to believe in all that the prophets have spoken! Was it not necessary for the Christ to suffer these things and to enter into His glory?' And beginning with Moses and with all the prophets, He explained to them the things concerning Himself in all the Scriptures" (Luke 24:25-27). At an earlier time in His earthly ministry, Jesus made an analogy to the prophet Jonah's experience as He alluded to His forthcoming death and resurrection: "For just as Jonah was three days and three nights in the belly of the sea monster, so will the Son of Man be three days and three nights in the heart of the earth" (Matt. 12:40).

When he was before King Agrippa, Paul also used the Old Testament to support his testimony of Christ's resurrection: "Having obtained help from God, I stand to this day testifying both to small and great, stating nothing but what the Prophets and Moses said was going to take place; that the Christ was to suffer, and that by reason of His resurrection from the dead He should be the first to proclaim light both to the Jewish people and to the Gentiles" (Acts 26:22-23).

Jesus, Paul, and Peter used Old Testament passages such as Genesis 22:8, 14; Psalm 16:8-11; 22; Isaiah 53; and Hosea 6:2 to attest to the credibility of the resurrection. Because of those and other scriptural references, direct and indirect, no Jew who trusted the Old Testament should have been surprised that the Messiah rose from the dead.

Paul twice in 1 Corinthians 15:3-4 used the expression "according to the Scriptures" as if to underscore that the resurrection was part of God's plan, not merely his own invention. We too can confidently direct people to the Scriptures' testimony—Old Testament *and* New—as we include the truth of Christ's resurrection in our gospel presentation.

The Eyewitnesses' Testimony

Over the centuries in western society, courts of law have accepted the honest, responsible testimony of eyewitnesses as a reliable form of evidence. Paul appealed to that kind of testimony in stating his third evidence for Jesus Christ's resurrection: "He appeared to Cephas [Peter], then to the twelve. After that He appeared to more than five hundred brethren at one time, most of whom remain until now, but some have fallen asleep; then He appeared to James, then to all the apostles" (1 Cor. 15:5-7).

Paul's comments are consistent with the fact that each of the Gospels says the risen Christ appeared to people (Matt. 28:9; Mark 16:9, 12, 14; Luke 24:31-39; John 20:14-16, 19-20, 26). The first apostle He appeared to was Peter (cf. Acts 1:21-22).

Paul gives no details concerning the appearance to Peter, but we do know it had to occur after Jesus' appearance to Mary Magdalene and before His appearance to the Emmaus disciples (Luke 24:34). Our Lord made a separate, special first appearance to Peter, perhaps because of the disciple's shame over denying Jesus and likely because he was a leader among the Twelve. Christ's appearance stressed His grace to Peter. Even though the disciple had abandoned his Lord, the Lord still supported him and forgave him. Jesus knew Peter would be His spokesman on Pentecost (Acts 2:14-36) and at crucial times in the following months and years (cf. Acts 3:12-26). Peter needed reassurance that his Master was alive and with him. Armed with such understanding, he would be a prime witness to the resurrected Christ (cf. John 21:15-17).

Jesus then made a resurrection appearance to the eleven apostles, who were still called "the twelve" even though the Holy Spirit had not yet selected a replacement for Judas Iscariot. That appearance occurred on the evening of the same day that He arose from the dead (Luke 24:36; John 20:19).

The apostles saw Christ in His resurrected body on several other occasions as well (Matt. 28:16-20; Luke 24:44-51; John 20:24-28; 21:1, 14; Acts 1:3), a fact that strengthened their credibility as those who laid the church's foundations (Eph. 2:20) and established its doctrines and practices through their teachings (Acts 2:42). The Twelve were certainly competent and trustworthy eyewitnesses to the resurrection.

If the apostles represent the *quality* of specific people who saw Jesus alive again in bodily form, the 500 brethren represent the *quantity* of eyewitnesses who saw the risen Christ. The apostle Paul does not identify those believers or write anything about the circumstances of Christ's appearance before them, but the early church likely would have known those people and believed their testimonies about seeing Jesus. Their testimonies to fellow believers would have been powerful statements verifying the truth of the resurrection.

Paul goes on to report that the risen Christ also appeared to one named James. That man could have been one of the two apostles named James, either the son of Zebedee or the son of Alphaeus (cf. Mark 3:17-18). However, I believe he was James the half-brother of Jesus, the one who wrote the Epistle of James and was a key leader of the Jerusalem church (Acts 15:13-21).

That member of Jesus' own earthly family—a man who, along with His other half brothers, originally did not believe that Jesus was the Lord and Messiah (cf. John 7:1-9)—became a strong and persuasive witness to His resurrection. Seeing that Jesus was indeed risen from the dead may have brought James to saving faith. Whatever the case, he was a believable and honest witness whom Paul included in his list of eyewitnesses to the risen Savior.

Paul's Own Testimony

The apostle Paul's fourth evidence for the truth of the resurrection was his own testimony as an apostle who did not see the risen Lord until after the other apostles. Paul was not one of the Twelve and in fact had long been an unbeliever—a zealous Jew who persecuted the church of Christ in its early days. Therefore his testimony as an eye-witness to the resurrected Christ was all the more extraordinary.

Christ's appearance to Paul was not only postresurrection but postascension, which makes Paul's testimony even more special and distinct. The appearance did not occur during our Lord's forty days after the resurrection but several years later on the road to Damascus (Acts 9:1-8). Later in his ministry Paul also heard or saw the risen Lord several other times (Acts 18:9-10; 23:11; cf. 2 Cor. 12:1-7).

Paul's description of himself as "one untimely born" (1 Cor. 15:8) indicates that he knew he came to faith too late to be one of the Twelve. The expression in the Greek usually denoted an abortion, miscarriage, or premature birth and was a term of derision for what-ever was useless, dead, or unformed. Prior to his vision of the risen and ascended Christ, Paul was spiritually useless, dead, and unformed—a person God could scorn. Yet Christ providentially chose to appear to Paul, save him, and call him to the high position of apostle. For all that, the apostle was compelled to express his hum-ble amazement: "For I am the least of the apostles, who am not fit to be called an apostle, because I persecuted the church of God. But by the grace of God I am what I am, and His grace toward me did not prove vain; but I labored even more than all of them, yet not I, but the grace of God with me" (1 Cor. 15:9-10; cf. 1 Tim. 1:12-17).

The powerful truth of the resurrection wrought three important changes in Paul's life. First, he recognized his sin and realized how far his life was from true godliness. Second, the risen Lord Jesus transformed him from being a persecutor of the church to being its greatest defender. Paul abandoned his self-righteous hatred for the cause of Christ and adopted a loving, self-giving attitude as he began to work tirelessly to proclaim the Gospel and plant the church. Third, thanks to the life-changing, supernatural power of the Gospel and the unmistakable truth of Christ's resurrection, Paul experienced a dramatic redirection of energy. As earnestly as he formerly opposed Christians, he now served and supported them as their leading teacher and spokesman.

The Common Message's Testimony

Finally, Paul testified to the resurrection's truth based on the existence in the early church of a common message: "Whether then it was I or they, so we preach and so you believed" (1 Cor. 15:11). Without exception, every genuine apostle, prophet, and teacher from the early church centered his preaching on the death, burial, and resurrection of Jesus Christ. And those great truths also should be at the heart of our evangelistic message to lost relatives, friends, and coworkers. Authentic Christianity, whether from the apostle Paul's day or ours, knows nothing of a gospel that does not proclaim and defend the death and resurrection of our Lord and Savior Jesus Christ.

PART THREE

TAKING IT
TO THE
STREETS

Chapter 10

THE GREAT COMMISSION

An unknown author wrote that on a dangerous seacoast where ship-wrecks were frequent, there once existed a little lifesaving station. The building was just a hut, and there was only one boat, but the few devoted volunteers kept a constant watch over the sea. With no thought for their safety they went out day and night, tirelessly rescuing the lost. Many lives were saved, and the station became famous.

Some of those who were saved, along with others in the surrounding area, wanted to become associated with the station. They gave time, money, and effort to support its work. They bought new boats and trained new crews, and the lifesaving station grew.

Some of those who volunteered at the station soon became upset that the building was so crude and poorly equipped. They felt a more comfortable place should be provided as the first refuge of those saved from the sea. So they replaced the emergency cots and beds and put better furniture in a new, larger building.

As a result, the lifesaving station became a popular gathering place for its volunteers. They decorated it exquisitely and began to use it as a club and even charged membership dues. Because fewer members were now interested in going to sea on lifesaving missions, they hired lifeboat crews to do the work. The lifesaving motif still prevailed on the club emblems and stationery, however, and there was a symbolic lifeboat in the room where club initiations were held.

About this time a large ship was wrecked off the coast, and the hired crews brought in loads of cold, wet, half-drowned people. Because these survivors were dirty and sick, they soon messed up the beautiful new club. So the property committee immediately had a shower house built outside the club where the shipwreck victims could be cleaned up before coming inside.

At the next meeting there was a split in the club membership. Most of the members wanted to stop the lifesaving activities altogether because they thought it was a hindrance and unpleasant to the normal social life of the club. Other members insisted on lifesaving as their primary purpose and pointed out that, after all, the club was still a lifesaving station. But those members were finally voted down and told that if they wanted to save the lives of various people shipwrecked in those waters, they could begin their own lifesaving station down the coast, which they did. As the years went by, the new station gradually faced the same problems the other one had experienced. It, too, evolved into a club, and its lifesaving work became less and less of a priority. The few members who remained dedicated to saving lives founded yet another lifesaving station. History continued to repeat itself, and if you visit that coast today you'll find a number of exclusive clubs along the shore. Shipwrecks are still frequent, but most of the people drown.

What a striking illustration of the history of the church! The work of rescuing men and women out of the sea of sin—of saving people from the breakers of hell—is the greatest work the church is called by God to do. Spiritual lifesaving is the essential priority for the believer on earth, and can only be done here. So why are so many believers either unwilling to engage in it or ignorant of the task at hand? The answer is not that complex—it's simply a matter of focus. If you want to put feet to all you've learned about the truth of the Gospel, you need to know what God desires from you as a witness in this world.

A MOST ESSENTIAL MISSION

If you took a survey of the average evangelical congregation concerning the primary purpose of the church, I believe you would receive several different responses, along the following lines.

A large number would rank fellowship first. Certainly the opportunity to associate and interact with fellow Christians who share similar beliefs and values is extremely necessary to survive in our evil culture. Some would consider sound biblical teaching to be the church's principal function. Since I have been called to be a pastor, I would never minimize the importance of expounding Scripture and strengthening believers in the knowledge of and obedience to God's revealed truth. Some members would consider praising God to be the supreme purpose of the church. And it is important—we are to exalt the Lord always.

All of those priorities are thoroughly biblical and should characterize every body of believers. But neither separately nor together do they represent the central purpose and mission of the church in the world. The ultimate purpose and motive of believers, both individually and corporately, is to glorify God.

The apostle Paul described salvation as being "to the praise of the glory of His grace" and later in the same letter declared, "To Him be the glory in the church" (Eph. 1:6; 3:21). Jesus Himself came to reveal and manifest the glory of the Father (John 1:14). Hebrews 1:3 declares Christ to be "the exact representation of His nature." Like our Savior, we are to praise, honor, and glorify our God in every dimension of life.

The supreme way God chose to glorify Himself in the realm of humanity was through the redemption of sinful men. Since the Fall, God has been drawing, is now drawing, and, until the final judgment, will continue to draw sinful men back to Himself—all for the purpose of bringing glory to Himself. When sinners are saved, God is glorified because their salvation cost Him the death of His own Son, the immeasurable price His magnanimous grace was willing to pay.

It is through participation in that redemptive plan that believers themselves most glorify God. Through Christ, God was "reconciling the world to Himself, not counting their trespasses against them," Paul declares; "and He has committed to us the word of reconciliation" (2 Cor. 5:19).

Our great mission in the church is to love, learn, and live to call men and women to Jesus Christ. As a believer who truly desires to glorify God and honor His supreme will and purpose, you will share God's love for the lost and share in His mission to redeem them.

Christ came into the world to bring sinners to Himself for His and the Father's glory. As Christ's representative, you are likewise sent into the world with the same purpose—to bring glory and honor to God.

If God's primary purpose for believers was loving fellowship, He would take us immediately to heaven, where spiritual fellowship is perfect, unhindered by sin, disharmony, or loneliness. If His primary purpose for us was learning His Word, He would also take us immediately to heaven, the only place where we can know His Word perfectly. And if His primary purpose for us was to give Him praise, He would take us to heaven, where praise is perfect and unending.

There is only one reason the Lord allows His church to remain on earth—to reach the lost, just as Christ's only reason for coming to earth was to seek and to save the lost (Luke 19:10). "As the Father has sent Me," He declared, "I also send you" (John 20:21). Therefore, a believer who is not committed to winning the lost for Jesus Christ should reexamine his relationship to the Lord.

Today we are blessed with incredible means of proclaiming the saving message of Christ. But like so many in the world today, many believers are frequently crippled by indulgent, self-centered preoccupations. As a result, they neither care nor understand that the Lord calls every believer to be an instrument in fulfilling the church's supreme mission. That is what the Great Commission is all about: "Go therefore and make disciples of all the nations" (Matt. 28:19). To make disciples is to evangelize, to bring men and women to Jesus Christ. Like the first disciples, when Jesus called us to Himself, He also called us to call others.

A MOST ESSENTIAL CALLING

God calls all believers in a similar way. First He calls us to salvation, which makes every other call to service effective. He then calls us progressively to more specific and ever-expanding service. The first men Jesus called were Peter and Andrew, followed by James and John:

And walking by the Sea of Galilee, He saw two brothers, Simon who was called Peter, and Andrew his brother, casting a net into the sea; for they were fishermen. And He said to them, "Follow Me, and I will make you fishers of men." And they immediately left the nets, and followed Him. And going on from there He saw two other brothers, James the son of Zebedee, and John his brother, in the boat with Zebedee their father, mending their nets; and He called them. And they immediately left the boat and their father, and followed Him.

—Matt. 4:18-22

When Jesus called those first disciples, He gathered together the initial fish-catching crew of His church. They were the first of the original band of evangelists He called to fulfill the Great Commission. They were His first partners in ministry. He had the power and the right to accomplish the work of proclaiming the Gospel all by Himself, but that was not His plan. From the beginning of His ministry, His plan was to use disciples to make disciples. His first call to them was, "Follow Me, and I will make you fishers of men."

That calling to bear fruit in evangelism is extended to everyone who belongs to Jesus Christ. Speaking of all Christians, Peter wrote, "But you are a chosen race, a royal priesthood, a holy nation, a people for God's own possession, that you may proclaim the excellencies of Him who has called you out of darkness into His marvelous light" (1 Pet. 2:9). Christ commands all of His followers to fulfill this duty and privilege.

A number of qualities that make a good fisherman can also help make a good evangelist. First, a fisherman needs to be patient, because he knows that it often takes time to find a school of fish. Second, a fisherman must have perseverance. It is not simply a matter of waiting patiently in one place, hoping some fish will eventually show up. Fishermen have to move from one place to another until they finally find fish. Third, they must have a good instinct for going to the right place and dropping the net at the right moment. Poor timing has lost many a catch, both of fish and of men. A fourth quality is courage.

Commercial fishermen, like those on the Sea of Galilee, frequently faced considerable danger from storms and various mishaps. Fifth, a good fisherman keeps himself out of sight as much as possible. It is so easy for us to get in the way of our witnessing, but that may cause people to turn away. That's why a good soul-winner, like a good fisherman, keeps himself out of the picture as much as possible.

That's because it is the Lord who empowers us to witness. And He also empowers us to train others to witness. In other words, He empowers His disciples to disciple, just as He promised in the Great Commission: "All authority has been given to Me in heaven and on earth. Go therefore and make disciples of all the nations" (Matt. 28:18-19). It is to that Great Commission we now turn.

ELEMENTS OF THE GREAT COMMISSION

In our Lord's final message, as reported by Matthew, Jesus mentions five explicit or implicit elements that are necessary for His followers to fulfill their supreme mission on earth. We become effective witnesses to the truth of the Gospel when we are available, worshipful, submissive, obedient, and dependent on God's power.

Be Available

Matthew writes, "The eleven disciples proceeded to Galilee, to the mountain which Jesus had designated" (Matt. 28:16). The first three elements for effectively fulfilling the church's mission are attitudes, and the eleven disciples implicitly demonstrated the first one by being where the Lord had told them to be.

As someone astutely observed many years ago, the greatest ability is availability. The most talented and gifted Christian is useless to God if he is not available to be used, just as God's greatest blessings are not available to those who are not present to receive them. Faithful discipleship always begins with simply being available to God.

Both before and after the resurrection, Jesus said He would meet His disciples in Galilee (see Matt. 26:32; 28:7, 10). He had called a large group of His followers for the purpose of commissioning them to reach the world, and now they were gathered at the place He had appointed.

We are not told who was present when Jesus gave the Great Commission, but it seems probable that it was the group of more than 500 that Paul mentions in 1 Corinthians 15:6. Because the Great Commission applies to all of His church, Jesus would surely have wanted to deliver it to the largest number of His faithful followers. Those 500 came with all their weaknesses, confusion, doubts, misgivings, and fears. They may not have been the most capable or brilliant people, but they were available and where the Lord wanted them to be. They were ready for service. Like Isaiah after his vision in the temple, they said, in effect, "Here am I. Send me!" (Isa. 6:8).

To be truly fulfilled in this life, you have to be available to God. Offer your time, talents, gifts, and resources to the Lord to be used as He would desire. Because the people gathering on the mountain were available, they had the privilege of meeting the resurrected Christ and being commissioned by Him, receiving promises of His presence and power.

Be Worshipful

"And when they saw Him, they worshiped Him; but some were doubtful. And Jesus came up and spoke to them" (Matt. 28:17-18). The second element implied here is the attitude of genuine worship.

The moment Jesus appeared and the disciples saw Him, they worshiped Him. When they saw the risen Jesus on the hillside, their confusion disappeared, and their shattered dreams were restored.

Yet, amazingly, some were still "doubtful." Matthew does not indicate who they were and what they doubted. It seems likely that the doubt concerned whether or not the person who appeared to them was actually the physically risen Christ. Out of that large group, only the eleven disciples and some of the women who had come to the tomb had seen the risen Christ before. Perhaps some of those in the back of the crowd could not see Jesus clearly and were reluctant to believe such an amazing truth without firm evidence.

As if to alleviate that doubt, Jesus graciously came up and spoke to them. Whatever the doubt was and whoever the doubters were, as the Lord came nearer and as His familiar voice sounded in their ears once again, their uncertainty disappeared. Then those who had doubted fell down and joined the others in worship. Their complete attention was on Christ. That is the essence of true worship—single-minded, unhindered, and unqualified concentration on Jesus Christ as Lord and Savior.

Be Submissive

Jesus then said, "All authority has been given to Me in heaven and on earth" (Matt. 28:18). The focus of Jesus' declaration here is on His sovereign lordship, but in context it also clearly relates to the believers' response to His rule.

Before the Lord gave the Great Commission, He established His divine authority to issue it. It is because of His sovereign power that His followers are to be completely and humbly submissive to His will.

The sovereign authority given to Jesus by His heavenly Father (see Matt. 11:27; John 3:35) is absolute and universal. He has authority to bring all persons before the tribunal of God and to condemn them to eternal death or bring them to eternal life (John 5:27-29; 17:2). He had the authority to lay down His own life and to take it up again (John 10:18). He has the sovereign authority to rule both heaven and earth and to subjugate Satan and his demons to eternal torment in the lake of fire (Rev. 19:20; 20:10).

Before giving the commission, Jesus had to first establish His absolute authority. Otherwise, the command would have seemed hopelessly impossible for the disciples to fulfill, and they might have ignored it. Without knowing they had the Lord's sovereign demand as well as His supernatural resources to guide and empower them, those 500 nondescript, powerless disciples would have been totally overwhelmed by the task of making disciples for their Lord from among every nation on earth.

Submission to the absolute sovereignty of Jesus Christ is not an option—it is our supreme obligation. We need to have the attitude, "Whatever the Lord commands, I will do." And that leads directly to the next point.

Be Obedient

Here Jesus gives the essence of the Great Commission: "Go therefore and make disciples of all the nations, baptizing them in the name of the Father and the Son and the Holy Spirit, teaching them to observe all that I commanded you" (28:19-20). This fourth element for effective fulfillment of the church's mission is obedience to the Lord's command, made possible only when the attitudes of availability, worship, and submission characterize your life.

The transitional word is "therefore." Because He is the sovereign Lord of the universe, Jesus had both the authority to command His followers to be His witnesses and the power to enable them to obey the command.

"Make disciples" is the main verb and the central command of verses 19-20. The root meaning of the term refers to believing and learning. In this context it relates to those who place their trust in Jesus Christ and follow Him in lives of continual learning and obedience. "If you abide in My word," Jesus said, "then you are truly disciples of Mine" (John 8:31).

The Great Commission is a command to bring unbelievers throughout the world to a saving knowledge of Jesus Christ, and the term the Lord used in this commissioning is "make disciples." The true convert is a disciple, a person who has accepted and submitted himself to Jesus Christ, whatever the cost. The truly converted person is filled with the Holy Spirit and is given a new nature that yearns to obey and worship the Lord who has saved him (Rom. 7).

Jesus' supreme command, therefore, is for those who are His disciples to become His instruments for making disciples in all nations. Those who truly follow Jesus Christ become "fishers of men" (Matt. 4:19). Those who become His disciples are themselves to become disciple-makers. The mission of the early church was to make disciples (see Acts 2:47; 14:21), and that is still Christ's mission for His church today.

The specific requirements Jesus gives for making disciples involve three participles modifying the main verb: going (rendered here as "go"), "baptizing," and "teaching."

The first requirement makes clear that the church is not to wait for the world to come to its doors, but it is to *go* to the world. The Greek participle is best translated "having gone," suggesting that this requirement is not so much a command as an assumption.

The second requirement for making disciples is that of "baptizing them in the name of the Father and the Son and the Holy Spirit." To baptize literally means to immerse in water, and various Jewish groups as a symbol of spiritual cleansing had long practiced certain forms of baptism. The baptism of John the Baptist symbolized repentance from sin and turning to God (Matt. 3:6). As instituted by Christ, however, baptism became an outward act of identification with Him through faith, a visible, public testimony that one belongs to Him.

Baptism has no part in salvation, but it is a God-ordained and God-commanded response to salvation. A person is saved by God's grace alone working through his faith as a gift of God (Eph. 2:8). But by God's own declaration, the act of baptism is His divinely designated sign of the believer's identification with His Son, the Lord Jesus Christ. Baptism is a divinely commanded act of faith and obedience. The call to Christ not only is the call to salvation but also the call to obedience, the first public act of which should be baptism in His name.

The third requirement for making disciples of all nations is that of "teaching them to observe all that I commanded you." The church's mission is not simply to convert but to teach. God calls the new believer to a life of obedience, and that means it is necessary to know what He requires. As we have already noted, a disciple is by definition a learner and follower. Therefore, studying, understanding, and obeying "the whole purpose of God" (Acts 20:27) is the lifelong task of every true disciple.

Jesus did not spend time teaching just to entertain crowds or to reveal interesting but inconsequential truths about God or to establish ideal but optional standards of obedience. His first mission was to make disciples; His second was to teach God's truth to those disciples so that they would live them.

At the beginning of their ministry with Christ, none of the disciples had a passion for souls or a passion for any part of the Lord's work. In fact, their response to unbelief was to call for instant divine destruction (see Luke 9:51-56). Passion came only after understanding and obedience. The disciples developed compassion, humility, understanding, patience, and love as they learned from and obeyed Jesus Christ. Obedience is the spark that lights the fire of passion. The way to develop a love for souls is to obey Jesus' call to win souls. As you do that, God will kindle that spark of obedience into a great flame of passion.

Lean on God's Power

Jesus concludes the Great Commission by stating, "I am with you always, even to the end of the age" (Matt. 28:20). While the first four elements for effective fulfillment of the church's mission are crucial, they would be useless without the power that the Lord Jesus Christ offers through His continuing presence with those believers.

A helpful way to keep your spiritual life and work in the right perspective and to continually rely on the Lord's power rather than your own is to pray along these lines: "Lord, You care more about this matter I am facing than I do; so do what You know is best. Lord, You love this person more than I do, and only You can reach into his heart and save him; so help me to witness only as You lead and empower. Lord, You are more concerned about the truth and integrity of Your holy Word than I am; so please energize my heart and mind to teach Scripture accurately."

Jesus did not simply command His disciples to *become* fishers of men but promised that He would *make* them fishermen for men's souls. As He later would make clear on more than one occasion, that promise was also a caution. Not only was He willing to make them into disciplers, but they could never be effective disciplers—or effective disciples in any way—without His power. "I am the vine, you are the branches; he who abides in Me, and I in him, he bears much fruit; for apart from Me you can do nothing" (John 15:5).

AN EXAMPLE TO FOLLOW

Both in Jesus' teaching and in His example we can see principles that every soul-winner must emulate. First of all, Jesus was available. It seems incredible that the Son of God, who had so little time to teach and train the slow-learning disciples, would be so open to those who came to Him for comfort or healing. But He never turned down a request for help.

Second, Jesus showed no favoritism. The poor and outcast could approach Him as easily as the wealthy and powerful. The influential Jairus and the powerful Roman centurion had no advantage over the Samaritan woman of Sychar or the woman taken in adultery.

Third, Jesus was totally sensitive to the needs of those around Him. He always recognized a truly repentant sinner. When we are sensitive to Christ's Spirit, He will make us sensitive to others and will lead us to them or them to us.

Fourth, Jesus usually secured a public profession or testimony. Sometimes He gave specific instruction, as He did to the man He delivered from demons (Mark 5:19). At other times the desire to witness was spontaneous, as with the woman of Sychar (John 4:28-29).

Fifth, Jesus showed love and tenderness to those He sought to win. Again, His experience with the woman at Sychar is a beautiful example. She not only was a religious outcast in the eyes of Jews but was an adulteress as well. Yet Jesus firmly but gently led her to the place of faith. Through her, many other Samaritans were saved (John 4:7-42).

Finally, in contrast to many of His followers, Jesus always had time for others. Some Christian workers are so busy with "the Lord's work" that they have no time for others, though that was a primary characteristic of Jesus' own ministry. Even while on His way to heal

Jairus' daughter, Jesus took time to heal the woman who had suffered from a hemorrhage for twelve years (Mark 5:21-34).

EVANGELISM AND SACRIFICE

Like the Christian life in general, soul-winning involves sacrifice. Jesus said, "For whoever wishes to save his life shall lose it; but whoever loses his life for My sake shall find it" (Matt. 16:25). In saving others, we lose ourselves; in losing ourselves in the task, we will be used to find others. If you want to reach the world, you must be willing to be rejected by the world, just as our Lord conquered death by yielding to death.

In a sense the life of evangelism involves sacrificing the greater for the lesser, the worthy for the unworthy. God's Word is clear that if we are committed to the salvation of those who do not know Jesus Christ, we will lose ourselves in order to reach them. Reaching the lost for Christ is difficult and demanding, and the results are often slow in coming and the rewards often delayed. Those to whom we witness frequently resent the Gospel, and even fellow believers may ridicule faithful witnessing.

In his devotional book *Quiet Talks with World Winners* (New York: Eaton & Mains, 1908), S. D. Gordon recounted the story of a group of amateur climbers who planned to ascend Mont Blanc in the Swiss Alps. On the evening before the climb, the guides outlined the prerequisite for success. They said that due to the difficulty of the climb, one could reach the top by taking only the necessary equipment for climbing, leaving all unnecessary accessories behind.

A young Englishman didn't listen and proceeded up the mountain with a blanket, a small case of wine, a camera, a set of notebooks, and a pocketful of snacks. On the way to the summit the other climbers began to notice various items left along the path—first the snacks and the wine, a short while later the notebooks and camera, and finally the blanket. The young man managed to reach the peak, but, just as the guides had predicted, he did so only after discarding all his unnecessary paraphernalia.

Gordon made this application to the Christian life: "Many of us, when we find we can't make it to the top with our loads, let the top go, and pitch our tents in the plain, and settle down with our small plans and accessories. The plain seems to be quite full of tents" (p. 55). The question you must ask yourself is: Are unnecessary accessories preventing me from fulfilling the mission God has given me?

Perhaps this true story will assist you in your answer. If you want to be a part of God's lifesaving crew, look at the example of John Harper, pastor of Moody Church in Chicago in the early 1900s and later a passenger on the *Titanic*. His character came to the attention of the Christian world after the sinking of that remarkable ship in 1912. Four years after the ship sank, a young Scotsman rose in a meeting and said he was a survivor of the *Titanic* and went on to tell his story. Shortly after the ship struck the iceberg, John Harper had leaned against a rail and pleaded with this young man to come to Christ. Later as the man drifted in the water on a piece of wood, he encountered Harper again, who was himself hanging onto a piece of wreckage. Harper again urged him to receive Christ. The young man refused. The tide brought Harper around again, and Harper asked if the man was saved yet. Soon after that, Harper disappeared under the water. That's when the young man decided to trust Christ as Savior. At the meeting he identified himself as John Harper's last convert.

Being a witness for Christ and the Gospel is a rewarding, but not an easy task, but it's one we are commanded to perform—even to our dying day. If you want to stand for nothing but the truth, I hope you'll be motivated to fulfill the Great Commission.

Chapter 11

HOW TO WITNESS

In the 1960s, while I was an assistant pastor at the church my father pastored, I learned an unforgettable lesson about what it means to be an eyewitness.

During one rather uneventful day, the secretary ran through the church door and announced, "There's a fight in the parking lot!"

Right away I went outdoors to see exactly what was going on. Not more than fifty feet outside the door, I saw a man lying in the dirt and two other men kicking and pummeling him. At that point I realized things were very serious, so I intervened.

"Hey, you guys, break it up!" I shouted.

When they didn't respond, I thought, *Well, maybe they didn't hear me*, so I shouted a bit louder, "Break it up!"

They still didn't respond, so I approached the men, only to hear one of them say, "Kill him! Kill him!"

Then I realized I was watching more than an ordinary fight—I was witnessing an attempted murder. By that point I could also see that the victim was a bloody mess. I couldn't even distinguish his face.

One of the assailants, a six-foot-five, 250-pound longshoreman who played rugby, looked at me and asked, "What do you want?"

I was momentarily frozen with fear because of the man's size, but I managed to say, "You'd better break it up and leave this guy alone!"

He pulled back his fist as if to hit me, so I instinctively began to retreat toward the church. As I backed up, both attackers came after me. I kept retreating, drawing the men away from their victim, until I stepped back through the door of the church. At that moment I said to myself, *They won't come into the church. I'd be able to have someone call the police.*

But when the two men barged on into the church, my dad, who

had been in his office studying all that time, came out and asked, "What's going on here?"

The big guy responded by taking a swing at my dad, which prompted me to yell, "Someone call the police!"

Suddenly the two assailants panicked, ran back outside, grabbed their injured victim, smashed his head against a wall, dropped him behind a bush, and sped away in a car. Meanwhile, I wrote down the car's license number, which I gave to the police when they arrived.

The beating victim was still alive but too scared to file charges against his attackers. He wouldn't even testify against them after the police caught them. So the court called me as a witness in the case.

I'll always remember what happened when I went to court to testify. At the witness stand the clerk asked me, "Do you swear to tell the truth, the whole truth, and nothing but the truth?" After I answered, "I do," an attorney instructed me to tell the court what I saw, what I heard, and what I felt. Those terms made me a witness because I actually saw the assault at the church and attempted to stop it.

WHAT IS A WITNESS?

Ever since that courtroom experience many years ago, I've equated a witness for Christ as someone who has seen, heard, and felt His power. Anybody who has a saving relationship with Christ is a viable witness for Him. As the apostle John wrote: "What we have seen and heard we proclaim to you also, so that you too may have fellowship with us; and indeed our fellowship is with the Father, and with His Son Jesus Christ" (1 John 1:3).

A witness is generally defined as "a person communicating testimony about something they have experienced." Legal courts want eyewitness testimony, not hearsay or testimony from secondhand witnesses. Information passed down through several sources is not considered valid or reliable testimony. Another courtroom analogy will further illuminate this concept and help us understand what it means to be witnesses for Jesus Christ.

A Witness Is Aware of the World's Courtroom

Even though Jesus is no longer living and ministering on earth, He is still continually on trial in the world's courtroom. And unbelievers are in effect the jury that is seeking to pass judgment on Christ and His claims. The Holy Spirit's task, as defense lawyer for Christ, is to convince the world that the Person and work of God's Son are true. And we are the witnesses the Spirit calls into the world's courtroom to testify on Christ's behalf.

Once you understand what a witness is, you'll know that people are going to draw conclusions about Christ based on your testimony. Therefore, it is essential that you and I realize that the Holy Spirit is calling us to testify for Christ in the world's courtroom.

A Witness Knows the Element of Sacrifice

Anyone who truly answers the summons to testify for Christ recognizes the element of sacrifice involved. And that should be true of you and me as we take the Gospel to people in our neighborhoods, our workplaces, and anywhere around the world. We can't expect to confront a godless, Christless society without sometimes receiving a negative reaction.

I once had the opportunity to speak on the topic "Christianity and Culture" at a large university near my church in Southern California. I decided to use the majority of my time to present what amounted to a gospel lecture. I knew the student audience was mostly unsaved, and thanks to the working of God's Spirit, several young men afterwards trusted in Christ.

But my talk that day also produced a number of negative reactions. Christian lecturers were henceforth banned from that campus; the free speech forum was shut down; the university no longer permitted students to have a Christian book table. The backlash to my talk really culminated a short time later when I spoke at a nearby college. A group of students that had protested my university lecture came over from their campus, surrounded the podium where I was speaking, and attempted to shout me down. They threatened to bomb the church where I pastor, and they made obscene phone calls to my home in the middle of the night, even threatening my wife and family.

Those experiences helped me understand a little more of what the apostle Peter meant when he wrote, "If you are reviled for the name of Christ, you are blessed, because the Spirit of glory and of God rests on you" (1 Pet. 4:14). To a small degree, I had experienced the kind of persecution the early Christians endured. But I surely fell far short of sacrificing as much as certain missionaries have.

One of those missionaries was John G. Paton, a nineteenth-century Scottish Presbyterian who went to a group of islands in the southwest Pacific then known as the New Hebrides to win the natives to Christ. Right from the outset it was a difficult and challenging assignment because those islands were inhabited by cannibals. Frankly, it was the sort of missionary call most of us would have resisted or that we would have asked God to fulfill by sending someone else.

But John Paton and his wife did not argue with God's will. When they arrived by ship, they had to row ashore and build a small lean-to. During their first weeks there, they stayed in that shelter and prayed constantly for a way to reach the cannibals with the Gospel. And God honored their faithfulness in prayer. Years later one of the native chiefs who became a Christian asked Paton who the soldiers were who surrounded his lean-to each night. God apparently protected the missionary with His holy angels.

During their first months on the islands, Mrs. Paton gave birth to a baby. Sadly, she and the baby died within a few days after its birth. John Paton buried them and had to sleep on their graves to prevent the natives from digging up the bodies and eating them. Those difficult circumstances brought him face to face with the hard choice of whether to stay or leave.

Paton decided to stay and near the end of his life made this incredible observation: "I do not know of one single native on these islands who has not made at least a profession of faith in Jesus Christ. When I first came, I heard the cry of cannibals; but as I leave, I hear the ringing of church bells."

That's the kind of end result we sometimes see if we are willing to sacrifice for the sake of the Gospel. Not all of us will be just like John G. Paton; but all of us can share the Gospel with others as God gives us opportunity—if we are willing to make the sacrifice. We need to remember that a hostile world is going to react against the Gospel and that we will be called on to pay the price—not just once or twice, but all the time—as we seek to be faithful witnesses.

WHY WE ARE TO WITNESS

With all the sacrifice and commitment involved in evangelism, and the heartache and disappointment that come when people don't respond to the Gospel, it is often tempting for us to be satisfied with praying, worshiping, reading the Word, and having fellowship with other believers. After all, we conclude, doesn't God sovereignly draw people to Himself anyway? However, it's wrong for us to think that we can excuse ourselves from evangelism, because God gives us clear-cut reasons to witness.

God Commands Us to Witness

The foremost reason we are to witness is because God tells us to. As we saw in the previous chapter, Christ's Great Commission in Matthew 28:19-20 is just as applicable to us as it was to the apostles. And we should also take to heart His exhortation to the disciples in Matthew 10:32-33: "Every one therefore who shall confess Me before men, I will also confess him before My Father who is in heaven. But whoever shall deny Me before men, I will also deny him before My Father who is in heaven." A sincere follower of Jesus Christ openly confesses Him before the world. Jesus' term "every one" includes all His disciples. They are willing to openly identify with Christ wherever they are, whether they are witnessing to just one friend or relative, whether they are leading an evangelistic Bible study, or whether they are responding to unbelieving coworkers on the job.

Someone once asked the influential preacher Charles H.

Spurgeon, "Mr. Spurgeon, since you believe in the doctrine of election—that certain people are elect for salvation—why don't you just preach to the elect?"

Spurgeon replied, "If you'll go around and pull up their shirttails so I can see if they have an *E* stamped on their back, I will."

Spurgeon's point was obvious: Since only God knows who the elect are, it is our responsibility to preach to everyone within our sphere of influence. A sovereign God will take care of His part in bringing people to Himself. The Lord wants us to exercise childlike faith and heed His command to "preach the gospel to all creation" (Mark 16:15; cf. Acts 1:8).

We All Have Sufficient Doctrinal Understanding

Even the most recent convert to Jesus Christ is responsible to be a witness for Him. God has commanded believers to be witnesses of His Gospel not because of all the theological expertise they have, but primarily because of what they have seen, heard, and felt in their saving relationship with Christ. And any believer, at any stage of Christian growth, can testify to those realities. You may know only that Jesus saved you, but that's enough to be an effective witness.

Each Sunday evening as part of our service at Grace Community Church, where I have been privileged to serve as pastor for more than thirty years, we have baptismal services. The testimonies of those being baptized are always powerful and very touching. But those people never speak in lofty theological terms or engage in profound doctrinal discussions. They simply describe what they were like before salvation, how God brought them to repentance and faith, and how He has changed them since.

Some of the testimonies are more dramatic, such as the former head of a Hell's Angels motorcycle group who went to prison on a second-degree murder conviction but then came to Christ near the end of his term. Some are more ordinary, such as those who tell of being good, moral people who were nevertheless living lives devoid of meaning or fulfillment until Christ transformed them.

No matter what the details of the various testimonies, they all bear witness to the transforming power of the Gospel. And they all demonstrate that witnessing begins with simple words about how Jesus can change lives. They are not concerned with expounding complex issues or answering difficult questions and objections. That concern becomes easier to handle as we grow in the Lord. But in the beginning it's important to declare the truth of a changed life.

THE ELEMENTS OF AN EFFECTIVE WITNESS

Along the way nearly all of us have experienced certain frustrations in witnessing. To begin with, we may have struggled with identifying the basic elements of good evangelism and knowing how they can make a positive difference in our overall testimony. But as you're about to see, those ingredients are not that difficult to recognize, and they are completely consistent with principles from God's Word.

The Corporate Testimony of a Pure Church

The corporate testimony, or reputation for spiritual integrity, of your local church is crucial to your individual witnessing efforts in the community. The purity of that testimony sets the foundation for how people will receive your presentation of the Gospel (cf. John 13:34-35).

A sinful corporate testimony from professed believers can have a devastating effect on evangelistic outreach. Suppose the church you attend is in turmoil because the pastor recently ran off with his secretary. Then imagine if the local media gets ahold of the story and publicizes it to the entire community.

Given that situation, it would be very difficult for you to share the Lord with someone at work, school, or down the street who knew of the scandal. Once you begin presenting the Gospel to that person, he could understandably cut you off by saying something like, "You go to the church where the pastor just ran off with the secretary, don't you? Well, I don't want to hear any more of what you have to say."

I think the point is quite obvious. The quality of the church's corporate testimony determines to a great extent how credible its members' individual testimonies will be. That's why it's imperative that believers have the kind of individual lifestyles that consistently honor the Lord (cf. 1 Pet. 2:12) and help our churches maintain pure corporate testimonies.

The Individual Testimony of a Pure Life

The purity of your individual testimony will have its greatest impact in your home as you live faithfully day after day and set a righteous example for members of your family. Unless they regularly see Christ's virtue and His character in your life, it will be very difficult, humanly speaking, to reach them with the Gospel. The same principle is true when it comes to winning neighbors, coworkers, and relatives for the Lord. The Holy Spirit remains the primary one who draws a person to Christ, but we must not be a stumbling block to that work.

First Peter 2:15 says, "For such is the will of God that by doing right you may silence the ignorance of foolish men." Many unbelievers want to slander Christianity, but our virtuous testimonies will shut the mouths of the critics, and perhaps be the start of their path to saving faith. You and I ought to strive continually, with the Lord's help, to have testimonies that are pure, that demonstrate to the world the blamelessness and consistent integrity of the Christian life. We can't live in sinless perfection, but we can live with an honest, upright sincerity that tells others, "Sure, I fail. But I turn to God, and He forgives me and helps me overcome my failures." That genuineness pleases Him and prepares the way for a third major element in effective witnessing.

The Recognition of the Holy Spirit's Power

An effective witness will also recognize that he or she is dependent on the Holy Spirit's power for fruitfulness. That important realization keeps you from manipulating people—such as those who may be emotionally agitated or psychologically vulnerable due to their spiritual need—as you share the Gospel with them.

Clever evangelists do not save anybody, although many have effectively conned individuals into making "professions of faith" in Christ. Scripture makes it clear that salvation is a supernatural work of God (cf. Jonah 2:9; John 1:12-13; 3:5-8; 6:44; Eph. 2:4-5; Titus

3:5). Luke cited an example of that truth in his Acts narrative: "A certain woman named Lydia, from the city of Thyatira, a seller of purple fabrics, a worshiper of God, was listening; and the Lord opened her heart to respond to the things spoken by Paul" (16:14). The apostle Paul preached the Gospel to a group of people just outside Philippi, and the Lord opened Lydia's heart to receive the Good News. It was not Paul's persuasive preaching that drew Lydia to salvation, but the work of the Spirit in her heart.

People have asked me if I get distressed when individuals don't always respond and receive Christ as Lord and Savior when I preach the Gospel. I tell them there is a sense in which I'm saddened and disappointed. But I also point out that God didn't call me to save people—He simply wants me to preach the Gospel to them. Saving people is His business.

If you or I have been faithful in clearly and prayerfully presenting the Gospel, that's all we can do. God does not want us to usurp the Holy Spirit's role (nor can we) and convince people on an emotional level to make a response that's not genuine. Instead, He wants us to entrust the results of our witnessing to the sovereign work of His Spirit.

The initial work of convicting men and women of sin, righteousness, and judgment definitely belongs to the Holy Spirit, as Jesus told the disciples:

> *"But I tell you the truth, it is to your advantage that I go away; for if I do not go away, the Helper shall not come to you; but if I go, I will send Him to you. And He, when He comes, will convict the world concerning sin, and righteousness, and judgment; concerning sin, because they do not believe in Me; and concerning righteousness, because I go to the Father, and you no longer behold Me; and concerning judgment, because the ruler of this world has been judged."*
> —*John 16:7-11*

In addition, only the Holy Spirit has the power to enlighten people spiritually. Paul quoted from Isaiah 64:4 when he instructed the

Corinthian church on this: "Just as it is written, 'Things which eye has not seen and ear has not heard, and which have not entered the heart of man, all that God has prepared for those who love Him.' For to us God revealed them through the Spirit; for the Spirit searches all things, even the depths of God" (1 Cor. 2:9-10; cf. vv. 11-16).

Unsaved people, by their own intellect, can't understand any of the blessings and benefits of salvation. Such understanding is available to them neither objectively nor subjectively; it's not something that can be grasped or inferred simply by human will and initiative. Therefore, when you're witnessing to someone, you have to allow the Spirit of God to do His work. When you do that, you'll be encouraged and rewarded to know that the Holy Spirit will use you in the lives of those who don't know Christ.

PRESENTING THE GOSPEL

Once we have a solid understanding of the definition of a witness, the primary reasons we ought to witness, and the essential elements that compose an effective witness, we need to know what issues must be included in a complete, scriptural presentation of the Gospel. In moving from the academic realm to the practical realm in witnessing, you must ask yourself, *If I want to articulate the Gospel as clearly and accurately as possible, what points do I need to be sure to include in any gospel presentation?* You'll find the answer in a core list of six truths that are clearly and thoroughly grounded in God's Word. In fact, as we list those truths and their sub-points, we will mainly let passages of Scripture simply speak for themselves.

The Holiness of God

The first thing an evangelistic presentation must make clear is that God is a holy God who demands reverential fear and respect. "The fear of the LORD is the beginning of wisdom" (Ps. 111:10; cf. Job 28:28; Prov. 1:7; 9:10; 15:33; Mic. 6:9). Much contemporary evangelism completely misses this point and instead begins with misleading statements about God's love and plan for someone's life. For unbelieving sinners the plan is disastrous eternally. We should respond to such thinking with a proper emphasis on the scriptural truths concerning God's holiness.

Because God is perfectly holy, His law demands perfect holiness. "I am the LORD your God. Consecrate yourselves therefore, and be holy, for I am holy . . . you shall be holy, for I am holy" (Lev. 11:44-45). "Who is able to stand before the LORD, this holy God?" (1 Sam. 6:20; cf. Josh. 24:19).

The New Testament also requires holiness. "Without [holiness] no one will see the Lord" (Heb. 12:14). "It is written, 'You shall be holy, for I am holy'" (1 Pet. 1:16).

A holy God hates sin, and therefore sinners cannot stand before Him. "I, the LORD your God, am a jealous God, visiting the iniquity of the fathers on the children, on the third and the fourth generations of those who hate Me" (Exod. 20:5). "The wicked will not stand in the judgment, nor sinners in the assembly of the righteous" (Ps. 1:5).

The Reality of Man's Sin

The second fact a good gospel presentation includes is the reality of human sin. Unfortunately, many popular evangelistic methods now de-emphasize or ignore the issue of sin. They offer "salvation" as simply an escape from punishment, a way to have a fulfilled life with wonderful relationships, and a promise of free forgiveness. Those are genuine results of salvation, but if in making them the primary appeal of our witnessing we fail to address sin, our message is seriously altered. To offer salvation to those who don't understand the seriousness of sin makes us little better than the false prophets of Jeremiah's day: "They have healed the wound of My people slightly, saying, 'Peace, peace,' but there is no peace" (Jer. 6:14).

All people, without exception, have sinned. The apostle Paul, quoting the Old Testament, makes this undeniably clear:

> *"There is none righteous, not even one; there is none who understands, there is none who seeks for God; all have turned aside, together they have become useless; there is none who does good,*

there is not even one." "Their throat is an open grave, with their tongues they keep deceiving," "the poison of asps is under their lips"; "whose mouth is full of cursing and bitterness"; "their feet are swift to shed blood, destruction and misery are in their paths, and the path of peace have they not known. There is no fear of God before their eyes."

—Rom. 3:10-18

Because of sin, true peace is impossible for unbelievers. "The wicked are like the tossing sea, for it cannot be quiet, and its waters toss up refuse and mud. 'There is no peace,' says my God, 'for the wicked'" (Isa. 57:20-21).

Because of sin, sinners deserve death. "The wages of sin is death" (Rom. 6:23). "When sin is accomplished, it brings forth death" (Jas. 1:15).

Sinners can in no way earn their salvation. "For all of us have become like one who is unclean, and all our righteous deeds are like a filthy garment; and all of us wither like a leaf, and our iniquities, like the wind, take us away" (Isa. 64:6; cf. Rom. 3:20; Gal. 2:16).

Sin renders all people helpless. "You were dead in your trespasses and sins" (Eph. 2:1). "There is nothing covered up that will not be revealed, and hidden that will not be known" (Luke 12:2). Also see Romans 2:16; Hebrews 9:27; and Revelation 21:8.

The Person and Work of Jesus Christ

The Gospel emphasizes both who Christ is and what He has done for sinners. If you desire to be an effective witness, you will always strive to keep those truths in balance.

Jesus is completely and eternally God. "In the beginning was the Word, and the Word was with God, and the Word was God. He was in the beginning with God. All things came into being through Him; and apart from Him nothing came into being that has come into being. . . . And the Word became flesh, and dwelt among us, and we beheld His glory, glory as of the only begotten from the Father, full of grace and truth" (John 1:1-3, 14; cf. Col. 2:9).

Jesus is Lord of all. "God highly exalted Him, and bestowed on Him the name which is above every name, that at the name of Jesus every knee should bow, of those who are in heaven, and on earth and under the earth, and that every tongue should confess that Jesus Christ is Lord, to the glory of God the Father" (Phil. 2:9-11; cf. Acts 10:36; Rev. 17:14).

Jesus became man. "Although He existed in the form of God, [He] did not regard equality with God a thing to be grasped, but emptied Himself, taking the form of a bond-servant, and being made in the likeness of men" (Phil. 2:6-7).

Jesus is completely pure and sinless. He "committed no sin, nor was any deceit found in His mouth; and while being reviled, He did not revile in return; while suffering, He uttered no threats, but kept entrusting Himself to Him who judges righteously" (1 Pet. 2:22-23; cf. Heb. 4:15; 1 John 3:5).

Christ's atoning sacrifice for sin makes possible the salvation of sinners. "He [God] made Him [Christ] who knew no sin to be sin on our behalf, that we might become the righteousness of God in Him" (2 Cor. 5:21). "In Him we have redemption through His blood, the forgiveness of our trespasses, according to the riches of His grace which He lavished on us" (Eph. 1:7-8). Other relevant verses you can share on this point are Colossians 1:20, Titus 2:14, 1 Peter 2:24, and Revelation 1:5.

Jesus rose from the grave. The angels at His tomb declared to the women who had come with spices and perfumes: "'Why do you seek the living One among the dead? He is not here, but He has risen. Remember how He spoke to you while He was still in Galilee, saying that the Son of Man must be delivered into the hands of sinful men, and be crucified, and the third day rise again.' And they remembered His words" (Luke 24:5-8; cf. 1 Cor. 15:3-4). "He . . . was delivered over because of our transgressions, and was raised because of our justification" (Rom. 4:25; cf. 1:4).

God's Demands of All Sinners

For them to be genuinely saved, it is inadequate that people merely "make a decision for Christ" or pray a "sinner's prayer" to escape hell and have a better life. More than that, God requires people to completely forsake everything else they trust in and turn to Jesus Christ as their Lord and Savior. That involves three profound changes of heart and attitude.

People must *repent of their sins*. "'Repent and turn away from all your transgressions. . . . I have no pleasure in the death of anyone who dies,' declares the Lord God. 'Therefore, repent and live'" (Ezek. 18:30, 32). "God is now declaring to men that all everywhere should repent" (Acts 17:30; cf. 26:20).

People need to *turn from idolatry and follow Christ*. "You turned to God from idols to serve a living and true God" (1 Thess. 1:9). "If anyone wishes to come after Me, let him deny himself, and take up his cross daily, and follow Me" (Luke 9:23; cf. v. 62; John 12:26).

People must *trust Christ as Lord and Savior*. "If you confess with your mouth Jesus as Lord, and believe in your heart that God raised Him from the dead, you shall be saved" (Rom. 10:9; cf. Acts 16:31).

Carefully Counting the Cost of Following Christ

Another reality that's crucial to include in your gospel presentation is some honest mention of the cost involved in following Christ. While stressing that salvation is absolutely free and includes everything people need for spiritual life, you also must tell them about the cost of discipleship that results from salvation. Obeying the Lord, like joining the army, can cost us our freedom, certain relationships, some independence, and maybe even our lives. A careful evangelist, like a good army recruiter, will tell potential inductees the full story. Christ Himself did not hesitate to tell people about the cost of discipleship:

> "If anyone comes to Me, and does not hate his own father and mother and wife and children and brothers and sisters, yes, and even his own life, he cannot be My disciple. Whoever does not carry his own cross and come after Me cannot be My disciple. For

which one of you, when he wants to build a tower, does not first sit down and calculate the cost, to see if he has enough to complete it? Otherwise, when he has laid a foundation and is not able to finish, all who observe it begin to ridicule him, saying, 'This man began to build and was not able to finish.' Or what king, when he sets out to meet another king in battle, will not first sit down and consider whether he is strong enough with ten thousand men to encounter the one coming against him with twenty thousand? Or else, while the other is still far away, he sends a delegation and asks for terms of peace. So then, no one of you can be My disciple who does not give up all his own possessions."

—*Luke 14:26-33; cf. Matt. 10:34-38;*
Mark 8:35-37; John 12:24-25

No Need for a Delayed Response

After you have carefully presented the preceding five components of the Gospel, it is time to graciously, sincerely, and with appropriate urgency encourage your listener to wholeheartedly embrace the message. Without question, you should never push anyone into a hasty response to your witnessing. However, you must make it clear that the Gospel contains far more than a collection of good ideas that the person can reconsider whenever he gets around to it. "Seek the LORD while He may be found; call upon Him while He is near. Let the wicked forsake his way, and the unrighteous man his thoughts; and let him return to the Lord, and He will have compassion on him; and to our God, for He will abundantly pardon" (Isa. 55:6-7). "Therefore, we are ambassadors for Christ, as though God were entreating through us; we beg you on behalf of Christ, be reconciled to God" (2 Cor. 5:20; cf. 6:1-2).

YOUR RESPONSIBILITIES TO A NEW CONVERT

If God should graciously use your witness to draw someone to Himself, you then have a new set of responsibilities toward that person. Evangelists in the church have customarily called that duty *fol-*

low-up. The apostle Paul's teaching to the struggling Corinthians contains some basic elements of follow-up.

Love Him or Her

First he tells them in 1 Corinthians 4:14, "I do not write these things to shame you, but to admonish you as my beloved children." The primary key to biblical follow-up is demonstrating a genuine love for the new believer. That love must go beyond warm, emotional feelings for the person and encompass the essence of Jesus' self-sacrificing action in John 13:1-17, when He washed the disciples' feet.

You can demonstrate practical love for a new convert by giving up some of your own time, priorities, and enterprises so you can invest in his or her life. Paul repeatedly showed such love for the various churches he established: "I will most gladly spend and be expended for your souls" (2 Cor. 12:15); "For God is my witness, how I long for you all with the affection of Christ Jesus" (Phil. 1:8); "We night and day keep praying most earnestly that we may see your face, and may complete what is lacking in your faith" (1 Thess. 3:10).

Admonish Him or Her

First Corinthians 4:14 also says that Paul admonished the believers at Corinth. The Greek word for "admonish" means "to put in mind," with the purpose of warning and reproving. One who did that sought to effect a necessary change—in belief, attitude, habit, lifestyle, and so forth.

If you are faithful in your responsibilities toward someone you have led to Christ, there will be times when you must admonish. You must not browbeat, humiliate, or proudly judge the other person; but you must lovingly and patiently criticize his or her wrong beliefs and behaviors and point him or her toward what's right (see Matt. 18:15-20; 1 Thess. 2:10-12; 5:14).

Be an Example to Him or Her

In 1 Corinthians 11:1 Paul declared, "Be imitators of me, just as I also am of Christ." It is critical that we not only be witnesses for Christ but also imitators of Him, and thus examples to new believers to whom we minister. That's why Paul was so confident and successful as a Christian and as one who mentored new Christians—he lived in such a way that everyone knew without a doubt that he loved and obeyed Christ.

Like Paul, you can be an example to those you have the privilege of bringing to faith in Christ. Simply place your life alongside theirs and live out the Christian life so they can see how it's done. If you're consistent and faithful, that is one of the most effective and practical elements of disciple-making.

Teach Him or Her

Finally, an important responsibility to any new convert is to teach him or her the Word of God. We must expound its basic truths, just as Paul and Timothy did: "He [Timothy] will remind you of my ways which are in Christ, just as I teach everywhere in every church" (1 Cor. 4:17). In the Corinthian church, Timothy was simply reinforcing by his own example and teaching what Paul had taught so carefully for many months (cf. Acts 18:11).

Undoubtedly, both men strove to make their teaching clear and understandable (cf. 1 Cor. 2:1-8), which is an essential trait for us to model. You and I must never omit or compromise correct doctrine, but frequently we must be willing to set aside theological jargon and just speak the truth plainly and in love (Eph. 4:15). The only way a new believer can know how he is supposed to live is by receiving Scripture-based input from us.

In John 15:26 Jesus told the disciples, "When the Helper comes, whom I will send to you from the Father, that is the Spirit of truth, who proceeds from the Father, He will bear witness of Me." There we see again that the Holy Spirit is in the business of witnessing to the truth of Jesus Christ. And it is our privilege simply to be the Spirit's instruments to communicate the Gospel to others: "And you will bear witness also, because you have been with Me from the beginning" (John 15:27). You can rely on His guidance and power as you fulfill your responsibility to evangelize the lost and follow up on new converts.

I trust that this chapter on the basic definitions and how-tos of witnessing has given you fresh motivation and the confidence that you can share your faith with the lost. If you work diligently to know and apply—even one at a time—the principles we've discussed, I believe God, who sovereignly saves all who believe, will be honored by your faithfulness in witnessing.

Appendix

"WHO DO YOU SAY THAT I AM?"

A Sample Gospel Presentation

[Author's note: The following is taken from a tract titled, *Who Do You Say That I Am?* Copyright 1991 by Grace to You. It is used here by permission of the publisher. Copies of the tract can be acquired by contacting Grace to You.]

"Who do you say that I am?" With that brief question (Matt. 16:15), Jesus Christ confronted His followers with the most important issue they would ever face. He had spent much time with them and made some bold claims about His identity and authority. Now the time had come for them either to believe or deny His teachings.

Who do *you* say Jesus is? Your response to Him will determine not only your values and lifestyle but your eternal destiny as well. Consider what the Bible says about Him.

JESUS IS GOD

While Jesus was on earth, there was much confusion about who He was. Some thought He was a wise man or a great prophet. Others thought He was a madman. Still others couldn't decide or didn't care. But Jesus said, "I and the Father are one" (John 10:30). That means He claimed to be nothing less than God in human flesh.

Many people today don't understand that Jesus claimed to be God. They're content to think of Him as little more than a great moral teacher. But even His enemies understood His claims to deity.

That's why they tried to stone Him to death (John 5:18; 10:33) and eventually had Him crucified (John 19:7).

C. S. Lewis observed, "You can shut Him up for a fool, you can spit at Him and kill Him as a demon; or you can fall at His feet and call Him Lord and God. But let us not come up with any patronizing nonsense about His being a great human teacher. He has not left that open to us. He did not intend to" (*Mere Christianity* [New York: Macmillan, 1952], pp. 40-41).

If the biblical claims of Jesus are true, He is God!

JESUS IS HOLY

God is absolutely and perfectly holy (Isa. 6:3), and therefore He cannot commit or approve of evil (Jas. 1:13).

As God, Jesus embodied every element of God's character. Colossians 2:9 says, "In Him all the fulness of Deity dwells in bodily form." He was perfectly holy (Heb. 4:15). Even His enemies couldn't prove any accusation against Him (John 8:46).

God requires holiness of us as well. First Peter 1:16 says, "You shall be holy, for I am holy."

JESUS IS THE SAVIOR

Our failure to obey God—to be holy—places us in danger of eternal punishment (2 Thess. 1:8-9). The truth is, we cannot obey Him because we have neither the desire nor the ability to do so. We are by nature rebellious toward God (Eph. 2:1-3). The Bible calls our rebellion *sin*.

According to Scripture, everyone is guilty of sin: "There is no man who does not sin" (1 Kings 8:46). "All have sinned and fall short of the glory of God" (Rom. 3:23). And we are incapable of changing our sinful condition. Jeremiah 13:23 says, "Can the Ethiopian change his skin or the leopard its spots? Then you also can do good who are accustomed to do evil."

That doesn't mean we're incapable of performing acts of human kindness. We might even be involved in various religious or humanitarian activities. But we're utterly incapable of understanding, loving, or pleasing God on our own. The Bible says, "'There is none righteous, not even one; there is none who understands, there is none who seeks for God; all have turned aside, together they have become useless; there is none who does good, there is not even one'" (Rom. 3:10-12).

God's holiness and justice demand that all sin be punished by death: "The soul who sins will die" (Ezek. 18:4). That's hard for us to understand because we tend to evaluate sin on a relative scale, assuming some sins are less serious than others. However, the Bible teaches that *all* acts of sin are the result of sinful thinking and evil desires. That's why simply changing our patterns of behavior can't solve our sin problem or eliminate its consequences. We need to be changed inwardly so our thinking and desires are holy.

Jesus is the only one who can forgive and transform us, thereby delivering us from the power and penalty of sin: "There is salvation in no one else; for there is no other name under heaven that has been given among men, by which we must be saved" (Acts 4:12).

Even though God's justice demands death for sin, His love has provided a Savior, who paid the penalty and died for sinners: "Christ . . . died for sins once for all, the just for the unjust, in order that He might bring us to God" (1 Pet. 3:18). Christ's death satisfied the demands of God's justice, thereby enabling Him to forgive and save those who place their faith in Him (Rom. 3:26). John 3:16 says, "God so loved the world, that He gave His only begotten Son, that whoever believes in Him should not perish, but have eternal life." He alone is "our great God and Savior" (Titus 2:13).

JESUS IS THE ONLY ACCEPTABLE OBJECT OF SAVING FAITH

Some people think it doesn't matter what you believe as long as you're sincere. But without a valid object, your faith is useless.

If you take poison, thinking it's medicine, all the faith in the world won't save your life. Similarly, if Jesus is the only source of salvation and you're trusting in anyone or anything else for your salvation, your faith is useless.

Many people assume there are many paths to God and that each religion represents an aspect of truth. But Jesus said, "I am the way, and the truth, and the life; no one comes to the Father, but through Me" (John 14:6). He didn't claim to be one of many equally legitimate paths to God or the way to God for His day only. He claimed to be the only way to God—then and forever.

JESUS IS LORD

Contemporary thinking says man is the product of evolution. But the Bible says we were created by a personal God to love, serve, and enjoy endless fellowship with Him.

The New Testament reveals it was Jesus Himself who created everything (John 1:3; Col. 1:16). Therefore He also owns and rules everything (Ps. 103:19). That means He has authority over our lives, and we owe Him absolute allegiance, obedience, and worship.

Romans 10:9 says, "If you confess with your mouth Jesus as Lord, and believe in your heart that God raised Him from the dead, you shall be saved." Confessing Jesus as Lord means humbly submitting to His authority (Phil. 2:10-11). Believing that God has raised Him from the dead involves trusting in the historical fact of His resurrection—the pinnacle of Christian faith and the way the Father affirmed the deity and authority of the Son (Acts 17:30-31; Rom. 1:4).

True faith is always accompanied by repentance from sin. Repentance is more than simply being sorry for sin. It is agreeing with God that you are sinful, confessing your sins to Him, and making a conscious choice to turn from sin and pursue holiness (Isa. 55:7). Jesus said, "If you love Me, you will keep My commandments" (John 14:15); and "If you abide in My word, then you are truly disciples of Mine" (John 8:31).

It isn't enough to believe certain facts about Christ. Even Satan and his demons believe in the true God (Jas. 2:19), but they don't love and obey Him. Their faith is not genuine. True saving faith always responds in obedience (Eph. 2:10).

Jesus is the sovereign Lord. When you obey Him, you are acknowledging His lordship and submitting to His authority. That doesn't mean your obedience will always be perfect, but that is your goal, and there is no area of your life that you withhold from Him.

JESUS IS THE JUDGE

All who reject Jesus as their Lord and Savior will one day face Him as their Judge: "God is now declaring to men that all everywhere should repent, because He has fixed a day in which He will judge the world in righteousness through a Man whom He has appointed, having furnished proof to all men by raising Him from the dead" (Acts 17:30-31).

Second Thessalonians 1:7-9 says, "The Lord Jesus shall be revealed from heaven with His mighty angels in flaming fire, dealing out retribution to those who do not know God and to those who do not obey the gospel of our Lord Jesus. And these will pay the penalty of eternal destruction, away from the presence of the Lord and from the glory of His power."

HOW WILL YOU RESPOND?

Who does the Bible say Jesus is? The living God, the Holy One, the Savior, the only valid object of saving faith, the sovereign Lord, and the righteous Judge.

Who do you say Jesus is? That is the inescapable question. His love compelled Him to die for your sins. He alone can you redeem you—only He can free you from the power and penalty of your sins. He alone can transform you, restore you to fellowship with God, and give your life eternal purpose. Will you repent and believe in Jesus Christ as your Lord and Savior?

STUDY GUIDE

CHAPTER 1:
THE CHRISTIAN'S DUTY IN A HOSTILE WORLD

Summarizing the Chapter

A fresh resolve to live for Christ in the midst of an increasingly hostile world, coupled with a scriptural anticipation of His imminent return, is a powerful incentive for Christians to evangelize the lost.

Getting Started (Choose One)

1. In your view, how eagerly do most Christians today look forward to Christ's return? Elaborate on your answer. How do you think you or members of your group could help others have a greater expectancy regarding the Second Coming?

2. Is it really more difficult to live as a Christian now than it was in your grandparents' generation? In the first century? Why or why not? What reasons do people in the church typically give for being unable to live as completely for Christ as they would like?

Answering the Questions

1. What two New Testament churches typify the contemporary attitudes of many in the church?

2. What are some of the general approaches today's evangelical churches have adopted in seeking to reach the culture?

3. Give a short definition of "easy believism." How has this teaching been harmful to a proper understanding of salvation?

4. What twofold truth does Peter exhort believers to remember when times are difficult?

5. Cite several verses that indicate we are now in the last days. When did this period actually begin?

6. How does the term "the end" in 1 Peter 4:7 refer to more than a simple cessation or termination?

7. Why is it best that we not know the exact date of Jesus' return?

8. How should Christ's imminent return affect the way you live? Give at least two Scripture references that support your answer.

9. Why is it important to obey the biblical injunction to guard your mind?

10. What quality is most fundamental for our witness to the lost?

Focusing on Prayer

• Examine your attitude toward the truth that Jesus is coming again. Do you live with excitement and anticipation, or are you apathetic, rarely giving His return much thought? Thank God that His Son will be returning soon, and ask Him to give you a greater eagerness.

• Pray that the Lord will give you continued or improved diligence in your daily spiritual disciplines so that you might set a good example for others in your family.

Applying the Truth

How fervent is your love for your Christian friends? Reread 1 Peter 4:8, and consider how it applies to your life. Memorize the verse, and ask God to show you a practical way you can strengthen a relationship with someone in your church.

CHAPTER 2:
OUR TESTIMONY AS SALT AND LIGHT

Summarizing the Chapter

People's lifestyles affect the lives of those around them. Therefore, as salt and light for Christ, we should be holy agents who help slow the world's moral decay and spread the light of the Gospel.

Getting Started (Choose One)

1. If an influence is truly worthwhile and effective, it will be noticed by those it touches, but it may not be noticed by those it originates from.

Was there ever a time when you had a positive or negative influence without initially realizing it? How did you eventually find out?

2. Is there a place for groups such as the Christian Coalition and Operation Rescue? Would you or have you participated in their activities? Why or why not?

Answering the Questions

1. What principle is illustrated by the two Greek myths at the beginning of the chapter?

2. What can we learn from the story of the missing Kansas farm boy?

3. What general failures will keep us from being the most effective salt and light to a sinful world?

4. What is the origin of the expression "not worth his salt"?

5. What ancient use for salt is comparable to the modern practice of notarizing documents?

6. Name at least three different meanings various commentators have associated with Jesus' use of the salt metaphor in Matthew 5. What is the primary comparison intended between salt and the believer's life?

7. How was Helen Ewing of Scotland so influential?

8. Summarize the main contrasts between spiritual salt and spiritual light.

9. God gives light to Christians in what two forms?

10. What are some challenges that threaten to render our salt and light ineffective and unfruitful?

11. What does Matthew 5:16 give as the ultimate purpose for our being salt and light in the world?

Focusing on Prayer

• Thank God for the privilege of being salt and light for Him in your community.

• Pray that God would keep your light shining for Him, even in the most difficult circumstances.

Applying the Truth

Learn what opportunities your community has for volunteer service. Prayerfully consider devoting some time to a charitable agency that's not a church or parachurch group. Look for opportunities to minister the Gospel as you serve alongside other volunteers and as you give assistance to those in need.

CHAPTER 3:
PRAYING FOR THE LOST

Summarizing the Chapter

We will not neglect praying for the lost if we understand what it is and why it's important and if we approach it with the right attitude.

Getting Started (Choose One)

1. Some believers persevere for many years in praying for an unsaved individual. What is the longest period of time you have prayed for someone's salvation? How did God answer your prayers?

2. If we don't understand why certain practices are good and important, we usually won't engage in them. What are some prime examples of that in everyday life? Which ones do people need to better understand the importance of and have a greater involvement in? Why?

Answering the Questions

1. Name two Old Testament and two New Testament figures who prayed for the salvation of others.

2. Why did Paul need to urge the Ephesian church to pray for the lost?

3. At what point should our prayers display the aspect of entreaty?

4. What is the only way the Greek word for "prayers" (1 Tim. 2:1) is used in Scripture?

5. What attitude does the word "petitions" imply concerning one who prays?

6. Name two passages that indicate what the scope of our evangelistic prayers should be.

7. What group is easy to exclude from our prayers for the lost? Why?

8. What general benefit results when we are obedient in praying for the lost? How does it specifically better our position in the midst of a hostile society?

9. What is the only reason a believer should be persecuted (see 1 Pet. 2:13-23)?

10. Why is it morally right for us to pray for unbelievers' salvation?

11. Regarding mankind's salvation, how is God's *desire* distinct from His eternal *purpose*?

12. List three or four verses that teach there is only one true God and one source of salvation. In what way is Jesus the only mediator (John 14:6; cf. Heb. 8:6; 9:15)?

13. How should knowing the design of Christ's atonement give us greater confidence in praying for the lost? Mention several reasons, along with supporting Scriptures.

14. What does the expression "holy hands" in 1 Timothy 2:8 refer to?

Focusing on Prayer

• Pray with renewed intensity this week for the salvation of someone for whom you have prayed in the past.

• Ask God to give you the kind of heart for evangelistic prayer that past role models such as John Knox, George Whitefield, and Henry Martyn had.

Applying the Truth

Examine the quality and frequency of your evangelistic praying. Reread and reflect again on the quote from C. H. Spurgeon at the beginning of this chapter. Ask the Lord to show you practical ways in which you can revitalize and improve your praying for the unsaved; then make plans to implement the changes.

CHAPTER 4:
WHO IS GOD?

Summarizing the Chapter
Evangelism must begin by proclaiming to unbelievers the truth of the one, eternal, unchanging, Triune God whose wrath is revealed against sin. But that same God, in His mercy, sovereignly offers salvation to all who believe.

Getting Started (Choose One)
1. Do you agree with the concept that scientific evidences and rational proofs are of limited value in pointing someone toward God? Why or why not?

2. Have you ever worked for a boss who was very fickle and unpredictable? If so, describe some of the frustrations that caused for you. How does having a steady, reliable employer make a difference for people?

Answering the Questions
1. What was Sigmund Freud's theory about God and man's relationship to Him? How was that view at odds with Scripture?

2. When it comes to a person's grasping the essentials of knowing God, what is the basic assertion he must make? What should he base that assertion on?

3. In what ways and with what terminology does the Bible indicate that God is personal?

4. What is an *anthropomorphism*? What is a key example of it in the Old Testament?

5. Why was it crucial for Israel in Moses' time to affirm her allegiance to the only true God?

6. What are two analogies people have used in attempting to explain the Trinity? Are such illustrations completely adequate?

7. How soon in Scripture is the fact of the Trinity clearly implicit?

8. What four important truths does the New Testament explicitly connect to the Trinity? Give a Bible verse in support of each point.

9. Name three times in redemptive history when God's wrath was poured out in a significant way.

10. What does Scripture consistently reveal about the general nature of God's wrath?

11. What is the main reason God is constrained to reveal His wrath against people?

12. What are the chief characteristics of God's plan of redemption (see Rom. 4:1-8, 11-12; 9:6-8)?

13. If God does not change (Mal. 3:6), how do we explain Genesis 6:6-7 and Jonah 3:10?

Focusing on Prayer

• Pray that the Lord would help your witnessing always to be God-centered.

• Thank and praise God for the truths of His Person and nature that you studied in this chapter. Pray that they would have a greater influence than ever on your personal testimony.

Applying the Truth

Memorize Romans 8:29-30. Write this passage out on an index card or small piece of notepaper, and put it in a place where it will remind you often of God's sovereignty in salvation.

CHAPTER 5:
THE RELIABILITY OF SCRIPTURE

Summarizing the Chapter

The Bible, as the inspired, infallible, inerrant, and authoritative Word of God, is the only reliable source of or standard for divine truth, moral conduct, and spiritual freedom that we have.

Getting Started (Choose One)

1. Without any regard for the Bible or absolute standards, try to write a

definition of *truth*. Do you think the average person today ever gives such an exercise any thought?

2. Do polls and marketing surveys have too much influence in modern life? Do you think their findings are really accurate or representative of what most people like and believe? How could such surveys be improved?

Answering the Questions

1. What sort of standards do unbelievers live by? How do most of them define acceptable behavior?

2. What does the Westminster Confession say about the basic contents of Scripture?

3. What verse most clearly spells out the doctrine of scriptural inspiration? What Greek word in the verse defines inspiration most precisely?

4. Briefly describe how God oversaw and guided the process of inspiration.

5. What do Jesus' words in Matthew 5:18 and John 10:35 indicate about the extent of Scripture's inspiration?

6. Have minor copyists' errors over the centuries affected the Bible's infallibility? Why or why not?

7. How do infallibility and inerrancy differ? What term conveys the similar, primary significance of both?

8. When did people really begin to abandon a high view of Scripture's authority? What trends in learning contributed to that abandonment?

9. What does neoorthodoxy say about the authority and content of Scripture? Why is it an inadequate, erroneous view?

10. What does Isaiah write about the Bible's effectiveness?

11. What facts about the authors of Scripture make it remarkable that the Bible has a consistent authority and a unified theme?

12. What reality do the biblical writers testify to more than 3,800 times in the Old Testament alone?

13. What confidence did the New Testament writers have in the Old Testament? In each other's inspired writings?

14. During His teaching ministry, what did Jesus always support?

15. What is essential in the life of any individual in order for him or her to embrace a correct view of Scripture?

Focusing on Prayer

• Thank God for His faithfulness in revealing and preserving a perfectly accurate and reliable Bible for your use.

• Pray for your pastor and all other teachers of God's Word, that they would maintain a high view of its contents and expound them accurately and with authority.

Applying the Truth

The Bible is truly a timeless book and definitely the most authoritative statement on divine truth and wisdom. If you are not already doing so, start a through-the-Bible-in-a-year reading program this week. (Follow any of several good printed schedules, such as those contained in the back or front of many Bibles.) If you have fallen behind in your Bible reading, resolve to spend some extra time in the coming weeks to catch up. (This reading program should be in addition to your devotional reading.)

CHAPTER 6:
AMAZING PROPHECIES

Summarizing the Chapter

Predictive biblical prophecy is a revelation of God and, as illustrated by prophecies concerning Tyre and Babylon, is always fulfilled and is therefore a trustworthy evangelistic tool.

Getting Started (Choose One)

1. Forecasting the weather is still an inexact science, even with today's high-tech aids. Has an inaccurate forecast ever affected your plans in a significant way? Share with your study group a particularly memorable instance of that.

2. If it were possible for you to know in detail all the future events of your life, what would you most want to know? Why? Would it be a good or bad thing to have such knowledge?

Answering the Questions

1. What does Henry Morris say to indicate the superiority of biblical prophecy?

2. Briefly restate the definition of genuine predictive prophecy.

3. Based on Deuteronomy 18:20-22 and Jeremiah 28:9, what is God's standard for true prophecy?

4. What multifaceted event constitutes the consummation of all Old Testament prophecy?

5. What made Bible prophecy so distinctive at the time it was uttered?

6. What two fields of study have repeatedly verified fulfilled prophecies?

7. What modern-day country was the city of Tyre located in? What was the ancient city noted for?

8. What six prophetic details about Tyre, included in Ezekiel 26, were historically fulfilled?

9. What nation laid siege to Tyre in 585 B.C.? Where did most of the Tyrians flee during that time?

10. Describe the military operation against Tyre that began the fulfillment of Ezekiel 26:12. What army was conducting the operation?

11. Who furnished the naval power to help complete the final campaign against Tyre? When was the island portion finally destroyed and by whom?

12. Briefly summarize the historical background and significance of the city of Babylon. What were its chief physical features?

13. What nation coveted control of Babylon and launched the final attack against it?

14. What chapter in the Old Testament describes events right before the fall of Babylon? Approximately what year was that?

15. Where are the ruins of ancient Babylon, and what have archaeologists observed about them? What prophet's words were fulfilled by those facts?

16. What is the mathematical probability that all the prophecies concerning Babylon could have been fulfilled merely by chance or coincidence? What does that mean practically?

Focusing on Prayer

• Thank the Lord for the richness of His prophetic Word and the perfect record of its complete and accurate fulfillment.

• Pray that God would guide you and grant you wisdom as you study various prophetic passages and seek a better grasp of their contents.

Applying the Truth

Do a special study of some of the prophetic chapters in Isaiah, Jeremiah, Ezekiel, and some of the Minor Prophets. Read them in several modern Bible translations, and use reference works such as a good study Bible, a Bible dictionary or handbook, and commentaries. Write down the subject, theme, the prophecy's extent, its original target audience, and so forth. Memorize the key points and verses well enough so you can use them in appropriate witnessing situations.

CHAPTER 7:
THE REALITY OF SIN

Summarizing the Chapter

Because every human being is born a sinner, the faithful witness will not sidestep the reality of sin's evils. Instead, he will follow Scripture and proclaim the only true remedy for sin's devastating consequences—the Gospel of Jesus Christ.

Getting Started (Choose One)

1. Have you noticed how leading politicians and top corporate executives, or their spokespersons, like to put a good spin on any news related to them, no matter how negative the news really is? Is such a practice honest? Does it frustrate you? Discuss.

2. In previous generations it was common to avoid talking about death and certain diseases. When people did discuss them, they often used euphemisms. Certain remnants of that attitude persist today. Do you think that's good? If not, how could people be encouraged to discuss such subjects more candidly?

Answering the Questions

1. What was the church father Chrysostom's greatest fear?

2. Sin disrupted what three basic human relationships (see Gen. 3:6-13, 17-19; 4:3-15)?

3. What is the simple definition of sin? List at least two other scriptural definitions that flow out of this one.

4. Mention some of the general metaphors that depict the defilement of sin. What are two specific ones the Old Testament uses?

5. What are at least two aspects of the rebellious nature of sin?

6. What Old Testament character is a classic illustration of the sin of ingratitude?

7. How does Isaiah 1:4-6 depict sin? What is the only remedy for it? Elaborate (see Matt. 11:28; Heb. 10:11-14).

8. What is original sin? To whom does it apply?

9. What components of the natural person's being does sin control?

10. How is the life of the typical unredeemed sinner like the story of Damocles?

11. What is the ultimate, most devastating result of unrepented sin?

12. Romans 6:23 expresses what two absolute truths?

Focusing on Prayer

• Is there a particular sin that you struggle with again and again? Pray in the spirit of Hebrews 12:1 that God would give you the discipline and determination to resist its temptation.

• Pray for someone you know who has so far rejected the Lord's remedy for sin. Ask that God's Spirit would yet cause that person to repent and be spared the horrible consequences of hell.

Applying the Truth

Ingratitude is one of the most prevalent sins, and it affects believers as well as unbelievers. Seek to cultivate a greater sense of gratitude over the next month by doing the following: First, make a list of all the blessings God has given you, and thank Him for each one. Keep a new list each week of all the things God does for you or graciously provides for you, and thank Him for each one; at the end of the month, thank the Lord for all He has done for you. Keep a separate list of those things you may have taken for granted, and pray regularly for those you will need in the future.

CHAPTER 8:
THE VIRGIN BIRTH AND DEITY OF JESUS CHRIST

Summarizing the Chapter

Christ's virgin birth was a unique event in human history, and its truth is essential to the Christian message, which says Jesus was both Son of God and Son of Man.

Getting Started (Choose One)

1. Do you think political parties would be more effective if members had to ascribe to stricter, more precise principles and ideologies? Why or why not?

2. The twentieth century witnessed many monumental events. Did any occur during your lifetime that should make the top ten list of the century's most significant events? What do you remember most about when they happened?

Answering the Questions

1. Name four miracle births before Jesus' time described in the Bible.

2. How long has the true church insisted on the virgin birth as an essential doctrine of the faith?

3. What Old Testament verse first implies that Christ's birth would be supernatural in some way?

4. What passage is the only Old Testament reference to the Father-Son relationship? What else does the passage contain?

5. What is significant about the Hebrew word for "virgin" in Isaiah 7:14? How does Matthew 1:21-23 support the intention of that verse?

6. In four separate references, how does Paul identify God in the Pastoral Epistles?

7. Briefly restate the logic, based on certain key Scriptures, that concludes with the truth of Christ's deity.

8. What additional truth about Christ does His deity lead us to conclude?

9. What was a major reason that Mary sought clarification of the angel's announcement to her about Jesus' birth?

10. What words in Mary's basic question to the angel indicated she understood what was going to happen?

11. What is the meaning of the title "Most High," as used by the angel to Mary?

12. What did Gabriel say to Mary about Jesus' identity that reaffirmed the Father's original plan for Him?

13. What further sign did Gabriel give to Mary to strengthen her faith in what she had just heard? In what ways did it confirm the truth of God's initial words to her?

14. What story in Genesis did the angel's words "For nothing will be impossible with God" remind Mary of?

15. How was Mary's final response to Gabriel's announcement a parallel to Hannah in 1 Samuel 2?

Focusing on Prayer

• Thank God for the truth of Christ's virgin birth, and ask Him to give you a better understanding and appreciation of its importance relative to Christ's deity.

• Perhaps you are facing a situation in which you need to trust in the Lord's sovereignty for a resolution. Pray that you might handle it in the faith-filled way in which Mary responded to the angel's announcement about Jesus.

Applying the Truth

As we have seen, Isaiah 7:14 and Matthew 1:20-25 are important foundational passages for the doctrine of the virgin birth. Write out and memorize these verses so that you may easily refer to them in defending the truth of our Lord's deity and virgin birth.

CHAPTER 9:
THE DEATH AND RESURRECTION OF JESUS CHRIST

Summarizing the Chapter

The death and resurrection of Jesus Christ form the essential climax of redemptive history. As such, it is absolutely necessary that we have a scriptural grasp of the historical and theological significance of those events. Otherwise, we will never be effective evangelists for Christ.

Getting Started (Choose One)

1. Do you remember when you first read or heard about the death and resurrection of Christ? Were you skeptical about their validity or unclear about their true significance? Recall your thoughts and reactions then.

2. Do you believe that contemporary people still have a good sense of history? Do our schools accurately and thoroughly teach history? Discuss which major events, concepts, and persons must be included in a good history curriculum or textbook.

Answering the Questions

1. What Old Testament verse is the first foreshadowing of Christ's crucifixion?

2. What did the Old Testament sacrificial system say about the importance of shed blood, and what future event did it picture?

3. What did the prophet Zechariah predict concerning Christ and the Jews?

4. Was the darkness during Jesus' second three hours on the cross local or universal? Does that affect the nature of its occurrence? What was the darkness most likely a sign of?

5. What was the theological meaning of God's temporary separation from Christ during the crucifixion? What was it analogous to in the realm of human relationships?

6. In addition to the cross itself, what was extraordinary about the way Christ's life ended? What earlier statement to the disciples did it fulfill?

7. What was the function of the temple veil? What was so significant about God's tearing it in two at Christ's death?

8. Name two special instances in which God caused earthquakes in the Old Testament. What did the earthquake at Christ's death preview?

9. To whom did the saints who were raised from the dead appear, and for what purpose? What does that miracle preview for all other believers?

10. What would be some of the consequences for Christianity if Jesus' resurrection were not historically true?

11. What have critics who don't believe in the resurrection never been able to explain concerning the "fabrication's" effect on believers?

12. While in front of King Agrippa, what did Paul rely on to bolster his testimony to the truth of Christ's resurrection?

13. What was the significance of Jesus' special postresurrection appearance to Peter, prior to revealing Himself to the other apostles?

14. What extraordinary aspects are associated with the risen Lord's appearance to Paul on the road to Damascus?

15. What three important changes did the resurrection work in Paul's life?

16. What was the early church's common message? How consistently was it in the center of preaching then?

Focusing on Prayer

• Spend some extra time praising and thanking God that Christ's death on the cross was sufficient to take away the sins of all who believe, including you.

• Meditate anew on the truths of our Lord's resurrection, and pray that your walk with the Lord would focus more on the hope and joy His resurrection gives to all believers.

Applying the Truth

Read the complete account of Christ's suffering, death, and resurrection in each of the four Gospels. Use a harmony of the Gospels if you have one. Compare and contrast the contents of each account. Based on that study, write your own summary or outline that incorporates all the details into one account. Use this as an aid in remembering all the key facts of the crucifixion and resurrection as a tool for sharing at greater length with someone who doesn't know Christ.

CHAPTER 10:
THE GREAT COMMISSION

Summarizing the Chapter

The church's supreme mission on earth is embodied in the Great Commission, Christ's call for the disciples to evangelize the nations. And we too are called to fulfill that mandate and bring men and women to Jesus Christ.

Getting Started (Choose One)

1. Have you joined the ranks of those people who sometimes or always work from home (the so-called telecommuter)? Do you ever have days at work that you feel could have been more productive at home? What projects are more effectively done at your home office? Why is that true?

2. Many of us hold on to material possessions we no longer need or seldom use. Does your garage, attic, or storage room contain such items right now? What two or three things do you most need to discard?

Answering the Questions

1. What are the main responses typical Christians give when asked what the primary purpose of the church is?

2. What should be the ultimate purpose and motive of all believers in all they do? In what context do Christians best accomplish that?

3. What Christian activities could be accomplished better if believers were taken to heaven?

4. In what twofold way does God call every believer? In what area of service does He desire all to be fruitful?

5. List four qualities of a good fisherman that also help make a good evangelist.

6. With what attitude does faithful discipleship always begin?

7. How many of Jesus' followers, including the apostles, were likely present when He gave the Great Commission (cf. 1 Cor. 15:6)? What would that suggest about the nature of its applicability?

8. Why would some have still doubted when they saw the risen Christ on the mountain?

9. What is the essence of true worship, as displayed by the group of disciples?

10. What elements does Christ's absolute authority comprise? Why was it necessary for Him to establish it prior to issuing the Great Commission?

11. What term did Christ use as the central command for the Commission? What is its root meaning?

12. What are the characteristics of the true convert to Jesus Christ?

13. How did Christ's baptism differ from John the Baptist's?

14. What sort of passion or zeal did the disciples lack in the beginning? What factors helped them fill that void?

15. List and comment on at least four of Jesus' six evangelistic practices—principles that any believer ought to emulate.

16. What overarching attitude did Jesus model in His ministry?

Focusing on Prayer

• Thank the Lord for the challenge of the Great Commission and for the spiritual resources He gives us to fulfill it.

• Ask the Spirit of God to search your heart and reveal things in your life that may be hindering you from fully obeying the Great Commission. Pray that He would help you lay those aside and serve Christ more sacrificially.

Applying the Truth

Memorize one or more of the following verses: Matthew 28:19-20; John 15:5; Acts 20:27; 2 Corinthians 5:18-20; 1 Peter 2:9.

CHAPTER 11:
HOW TO WITNESS

Summarizing the Chapter

When Christians realize they are witnesses for Christ and are motivated by the biblical reasons to witness, they will learn to clearly articulate the essential elements and key issues of the Gospel when they witness. They will also be faithful in their follow-up responsibilities to any new converts.

Getting Started (Choose One)

1. Have you ever considered the truth of the old saying that eyewitnesses to the same incident can view it very differently? This seems especially true concerning a traffic accident or a crime. Have you ever had to sort out the conflicting accounts of such an event? How difficult was it? What was the final resolution?

2. It can be frustrating when our children, our subordinates or coworkers on the job, or others ask us why they ought to do something we've requested of them. Is it always best to provide them with a reason? Do you think people are more productive and effective when they know the reason for doing something?

Answering the Questions

1. Define a witness for Christ (see 1 John 1:3). How is that similar to the general definition of a witness?

2. What role does the Holy Spirit assume on behalf of Christ? What does the Spirit call believers to testify to?

3. What fruit did missionary John G. Paton realize from his willingness to sacrifice for the sake of spreading the Gospel?

4. What is the primary reason we are supposed to witness for Christ? Support your answer with at least two Bible verses.

5. What constitutes sufficient doctrinal understanding to be a good witness?

6. What foundation does the pure testimony of a local church lay?

7. Where is the impact of a pure individual testimony the greatest?

8. What unscriptural methodology do we avoid in our witnessing if we remember we're completely dependent on the Holy Spirit's power for results?

9. What does Scripture make clear about the nature of salvation? Cite at least three verses that prove this.

10. What is involved when the Holy Spirit enlightens people spiritually?

11. What does God demand as a result of His holiness? What four Scripture verses demonstrate this?

12. List five facts or consequences, along with supporting Scriptures, related to the reality of man's sin.

13. What are six truths we must not fail to tell people regarding the Person and work of Jesus Christ? Give at least one Scripture reference for each.

14. What three profound changes of heart and attitude does God demand of anyone who would be genuinely saved?

15. What did Jesus conclude in His teaching about counting the cost of discipleship?

16. What Old Testament prophetic verses exhort sinners not to delay in turning to the Lord?

17. Reiterate the four basic elements of follow-up that are our responsibilities after God allows us to lead someone to Christ.

Focusing on Prayer

• Pray that God would give you confidence in how to balance the use of doctrinal truths in your witnessing—not to hesitate in your witness simply because you haven't studied much doctrine yet, and not to engage in overly complex theological discussions at the expense of a clear gospel presentation.

• Pray that your personal testimony would be all it should be to please the Lord and contribute to a pure corporate testimony by your local church.

Applying the Truth

Be sure you have a good understanding and firm grasp of the concepts we discussed under "Taking It to the Streets." If these are new and unfamiliar to you, carefully review and study them so you will know them by heart in the next two or three months. Go over each part with a mature believer to test your comprehension. Then pray for opportunities to share them with the lost. If you already know the principles well, ask the Lord for an opportunity to present them to an unbeliever sometime during the coming month.

SCRIPTURE INDEX

Genesis

1:1	54
1:1—2:3	54
1:2	109
1:26	54
3	116
3:6-13	90
3:8	49
3:8-24	97
3:15	79, 104, 116
3:17-19	90
3—4	90
4:3-15	90
6:6-7	61
6:7	57
9:4	71
11:7	54
12:1-3	104
15:6	60
18:9-14	101
18:10-14	111
18:14	111
21:1-2	101
22:8, 14	126

Exodus

9:16	64
10:14-15	118
12	116
19:18	121
20:4-5	53
20:5	157
32:12	58
32:14	61

Leviticus

2:13	28
11:44-45	157
17:11	71
26:27	92

Numbers

14:19	36
23:19	61
25:3	58

Deuteronomy

4:35, 39	44
6:4	44, 53
6:13	107
18:20-22	79
25:4	72

Joshua

1:8	22
10:12-13	118
24:19	157

Judges

13:2-5, 24	101, 102

1 Samuel

1:11, 18	112
1:11, 19-20	102
1—2	112
6:20	157
7:3-5	36
15:11	61
27:1	62

2 Samuel

15:7—17:4	93
22:2-3	62

1 Kings

8:22	46
8:38	92
8:46	166
13:2	80
19:11	121

2 Kings

5:27	95
20:9-11	119
23:15-20	80

1 Chronicles

14:1	81

2 Chronicles

2:16	82
13:5	28

Nehemiah

8:6	46

Job

5:7	97
26:7	70
28:28	156
38:4-7	50

Psalms

1:5	157
2	105
2:7	55, 110
2:7-9	104
2:8-9	105
7:11	58
7:14	94
16:8-11	126
19:7	66, 71
22	126
32:1-2	99
33:6	64
51:5	95
66:18	46
89:13	52
103:19	168
111:10	156
115:3	111
119:89	64
119:81	71
119:105	30
119:140	71
119:142	71
119:151	71
119:152	71
134:2	46
145:8-9	43
148	59

Proverbs

1:7	156
4:16	94
9:10	156
10:12	23
15:33	156
23:7	21
30:5	66, 67

Ecclesiastes

1:2	97

Isaiah

1:4-6	94
1:15	46
6:3	166
6:8	139
7:14	105, 106
13:3—14:23	84
13:10-11	118
13:19-22	84, 87
14:12-21	92
14:23	84, 87
14:24	62
30:22	91
41:21-23	78
43:10	44
43:11	106
43:14	107
44:6	44, 53
44:28	80
45:5-6, 21-22	44
45:22	106
45:23	107
46:9	44
46:9-10	45, 78
48:16	55
50:2	52
52:13—53:10	116
53	126
53:5	119
53:11	116
53:12	46
55:6-7	161
55:7	168
55:10-11	69
57:20-21	158
64:4	155
64:6	158
65:16	67

Jeremiah

6:14	156
9:5	94
10:10	67
13:23	93
17:9	96
26:3	61
28:9	78
29:13	51
32:17	111
44:16-17	96
50:1—51:58	84
51:26	87
51:26, 43	84
51:43	87

Ezekiel

18:4	167

18:30, 32	160
20:43	92
24:12	94
25:1—32:32	82
26	82
26:3-4	82, 83
26:4-5	83
26:4, 14	82
26:5, 14	82
26:7-8	82
26:8	82
26:12	82, 83
26:14	82, 83
26—28	82
27:3	82
29:17-20	82
33:11	39, 42

Daniel

4:35	111
5:1-12, 17-31	87
9:27	29

Hosea

6:2	126
13:14	107

Joel

2:2	118

Amos

3:7	71

Jonah

2:9	154
3:10	61

Micah

5:2	81
6:9	156

Zephaniah

1:14-15	118

Zechariah

3:3	92
4:10	52
12:10	116

Malachi

3:6	60

Matthew

1:20	106
1:20-25	113
1:21	106
1:21-23	105
3:6	142
3:7-12	97
3:13-17	56
4:18-22	137
4:19	141
5	32
5:13	28, 32
5:13-14	26, 27
5:13-16	26
5:14	30, 31
5:15	32
5:16	32, 33
5:17	73
5:18	65
5:45	44, 93
8:12	118
9:37-38	15
10:32-33	151
10:34-38	161
11:2-6	80
11:27	140
11:28	95
12:40	126
16:15	165
16:25	145
18:15-20	162
22:13	118
22:14	45
23:37	43
24:2	18
24:35	64
24:36	20
24:42	22
24:42-44	21
25:30	118
26:24, 54	73
26:32	138
26:41	22
27:45	118
27:45-53	117
27:46	119
27:50	120
27:51	18, 121
27:52	122
27:53	122
28:7, 10	138
28:9	127
28:16	138
28:16-20	128
28:17-18	139
28:18	140
28:18-19	138
28:18-20	15

28:19	56, 136
28:19-20	151
28:20	143

Mark

1:9-11	56
3:17-18	128
5:19	144
5:21-34	145
8:31	123
8:35-37	161
9:9, 31	123
11:22	62
12:29-30	53
15:25	117
15:43-45	120
16:9, 12, 14	127
16:15	45, 152

Luke

1	107, 109
1:5-17	102
1:29-30	109
1:30-35	104
1:31-33	109
1:34-38	108
1:35	55
1:36	110
1:37	111
1:38	112
1:39-40	111
1:48	112
1:68	107
1:79	31
2:11	106
3	105
3:7-9	97
3:21-22	56
9:23	160
9:51-56	143
9:62	160
10:7	72
12:2	158
12:37	21
14:26-33	161
16:17	73
18:31	73
19:10	136
23:34	46, 118
23:43	118
23:45	118
23:46	120
24:5-8	159
24:25-27	126

24:26-27, 44-47	73
24:31-39	127
24:34	127
24:36	128
24:44-51	128

John

1:1-2	110
1:1-3, 14	158
1:3	168
1:5, 9	31
1:9	27, 31
1:12-13	154
1:14	135
1:14, 18	52
3:5-8	74, 154
3:16	23, 44, 167
3:19	96
3:33	67
3:35	140
3:36	97
4:7-42	144
4:24	52
4:28-29	144
5:18	166
5:27-29	140
5:39	73
6:37	62
6:44	154
7:1-9	128
8:31	141, 168
8:31-32	75
8:44	97
8:46	166
9:5	27
10:18	56, 120, 140
10:27-28	31
10:30	165
10:30, 38	53
10:33	166
10:35	65, 73
11:25	124
12:24-25	161
12:26	160
12:45	53
13:1-17	162
13:34-35	153
13:35	23
14:6	44, 168
14:7-10	53
14:15	168
14:16-17	56
15:5	144
15:26	163

15:27	163
16:7-11	155
17:2	140
17:3	67
17:6	43
17:11	53
17:12	45
17:15-16, 18	25
19:7	166
19:26-27	118
19:30	120
20:14-16, 19-20, 26	127
20:19	128
20:21	136
20:24-28	128
21:1, 14	128
21:15-17	128

Acts

1:3	128
1:7	20
1:8	152
1:21-22	127
2:14-36	124, 127
2:42	128
2:47	142
3:12-26	124, 127
3:26	39
4:12	44, 106, 167
7:59-60	36
7:60	46
9:1-8	129
10:36	159
10:43	44
13:48	45
14:17	44
14:21	142
15:13-21	128
16:14	155
16:31	160
17:28	93
17:30	39, 160
17:30-31	168, 169
18:9-10	129
18:11	163
20:27	142
23:11	129
26:20	160
26:22-23	126

Romans

1:4	159, 168
1:18	57, 59
1:18-21	58

1:18-32	15, 43
1:19-20	49, 93
1:21	59
1:24-32	94
1:28	50
2:8-9	58
2:14-15	91
2:16	158
3:9-12	95
3:10-12	167
3:10-18	158
3:20	158
3:21-26	44
3:23	95, 166
3:26	167
3:29-30	53
4	59
4:4-8	32
4:7-8	99
4:11-12	60
4:25	119, 159
5:1	44
5:8	23
5:12	95
6:4	56
6:16	97
6:23	90, 98, 158
7	141
7:12	91
7:15-25	32
7:19, 23	95
8:11	56
8:18-22	97
8:26	38
8:29-30	60
9	59
9:1-4	36
9:3	42
9:6-8	60
9:11-12	59
9:17	65
9:22-23	43
10:1	36, 42
10:9	124, 160, 168
10:14	74
11:33-36	43
12:1	96
13:1-5	40
14:23	90
15:4	71

1 Corinthians

1:2	45
1:10	125

1:21-24	74
1:7-8	56
2:1	125
2:1-8	163
2:9-10	156
2:10-16	75
2:11-16	156
2:14	96
3:1	125
4:14	162
4:17	163
8:4, 6	44
8:4-6	53
9:27	32
10:1	125
10:31	59
11:1	162
15:1	125
15:1-2	125
15:3	119
15:3-4	126, 127, 159
15:5-7	127
15:6	139
15:8	129
15:9-10	129
15:11	130
15:19	124
15:20	122
16:22	97

2 Corinthians

1:21-22	56
2:14	45
2:14-16	33
4:6	31
4:15	38
5:9-10	20
5:17	32
5:19	135
5:20	161
5:21	119, 159
6:1-2	161
7:1	92
10:3-5	10
10:4	40
10:5	22
12:1-7	129
12:15	162

Galatians

1:1	56
2:16	158
3:7	60
3:8	64
3:10	97
3:13	107, 117, 119
3:16	104
3:22	64

Ephesians

1:3-14	32
1:4-5	42
1:6	135
1:7-8	159
1:13	56
2	97
2:1	158
2:1-2	97
2:1-3	166
2:3	97
2:4	23
2:4-5	154
2:8	142
2:8-9	98
2:10	169
2:20	128
3:21	135
4:15	163
4:17-19	96
5:8	28

Philippians

1:8	162
1:16-17	11
2:2	23
2:6-7	159
2:8-11	122
2:9-11	107, 159
2:10-11	168
2:15	31
3:14	20
4:8	22

Colossians

1:13	28
1:16	168
1:20	159
2:9	158, 166
3:2	21
3:14	23
3:16	22

1 Thessalonians

1:5	70
1:8	45
1:9	160
1:9-10	19
1:10	97
2:10-12	162

3:10	162
4:11	41
4:16	122
4:17	17
5:14	162

2 Thessalonians

1:7-9	169
1:8-9	166
2:7-12	29
3:11-12	41

1 Timothy

1:12-17	129
1:17	52
2:1	37
2:1-2	39
2:1-8	36
2:2	39, 40, 41
2:3	42
2:3-4	106
2:3-7	42
2:4	43
2:5	44, 53
2:6	45
2:8	45
4:1	18
4:10	45
5:18	72

2 Timothy

3:1-5	18
3:15	65
3:16	64
4:8	20

Titus

1:2	67
1:15	94
2:10, 13	106
2:11	39
2:11-12	22
2:13	167
2:14	159
3:1-2	40
3:1-3	40
3:4	106
3:5	154, 155

Hebrews

1:1	71
1:3	110, 135
1:6	107
4:15	159, 166

4:16	121
6:18	67
7:25	38
8:6	44
9:11-14	94
9:14	56
9:15	44
9:26-28	18
9:27	158
9:28	117
10:4	116
10:11-14	94
10:14-22	18
10:29	92
11:6	50
12:1	96
12:14	157
12:24	44
12:26-27	122

James

1:13	166
1:15	158
1:17	60
2:19	168
4:17	90
5:7-8	19

1 Peter

1:1-2	56
1:3	56
1:5	19
1:7	19
1:10-11	80
1:16	157, 166
1:18-19	107
1:18-21	44
1:25	64
2:9	33, 137
2:11	11
2:12	11, 154
2:13-23	40
2:15	11, 154
2:17	40
2:22-23	159
2:24	119, 159
3:15	11
3:18	117, 119, 167
4:7	18, 21, 22
4:7-8	17
4:8	23
4:14	150

2 Peter

1:3-4	32
1:21	65, 71
2:4	118
3:14, 18	24
3:15-16	72

1 John

1:3	148
1:5-7	30
1:7	116
2:15	25
2:15-16	96
2:18	18
2:28	20
3:2-3	20
3:4	90
3:5	159
4:10	119
4:14	45
4:19	23
5:17	90
5:19	97
5:20	67

Jude

6	118

Revelation

1:5	159
2:4	15
3:15-16	15
5:9	117
5:9-10	122
6—19	29
6:12	122
6:12-14	61
8:5	122
8:7-11	61
8:12	61
11:13	12
13:8	117
16:18	122
17:14	159
19:9	72
19:20	140
20:10	140
20:11-15	98
21:5	72
21:8	158
22:17	45

GENERAL INDEX

Abraham, 59, 60, 64, 101, 111
Absalom, 93
Absolutes, moral, 61, 63, 68
Adam, 57, 95, 116
   Adam and Eve, 57, 116
Agrippa, 126
Alexander the Great, 82, 83
"Amazing Grace" (John Newton), 17
Andrew, 136, 137
Anthropomorphisms, 52
Atheism, 9
Atonement, 44, 45, 54, 121
Attributes of God, The (Pink), 50, 52, 55, 59, 61

Babylon, 80-85, 87
Bainton, Roland H., 125
Baptism, 9, 55, 123, 142, 152
Basic Christian Doctrines (Henry, editor), 103
Belshazzar, 85-87
Bible Prophecies Fulfilled Today (Davis), 87
Brown, Louise, 101
Bruce, F. F., 102

Cain and Abel, 90
Chapman, J. Wilbur, 89
Chantry, Walter, 49
Chicago Statement on Biblical Inerrancy, 67
Christians as light, 12, 25 (Chapter 2 passim)
Christians as salt, 12, 25 (Chapter 2 passim)
Chrysostom, 89
Culture war, the, 10, 40
Cyrus, 80

Damocles, 97
Daniel, 70, 85-87
David, 62, 80-82, 93, 103, 105
Davis, George, 87
Deity of Jesus Christ, the, 12, 53, 59, 101 (Chapter 8 passim), 165, 166, 168
Dilley sextuplets, 101
Dionne quintuplets, 101

Early Christianity (Bainton), 126
Elizabeth, 102, 108, 110, 111
Ewing, Helen, 29, 30
Explorations in Bible Lands in the Nineteenth Century (Kilprect), 87

Fischer quintuplets, 101
Flavel, John, 94
Follow-up, 161, 162
Freud, Sigmund, 49, 50

Gabriel, the angel, 104, 105, 109, 111, 112
Gehazi, 95
Gordon, S. D., 145, 146
Gospel According to Matthew, The (Morgan), 26
Great Commission, the, 15, 133 (Chapter 10 passim), 151

Hannah, 102, 112
Harper, John, 146
Harvey, William, 71
Herodotus, 84
Hodge, Charles, 52, 53
Holiness, holy living, 24, 46, 92, 156, 157, 166-168

Inerrancy of the Scriptures, 67, 77

Infallibility of the Scriptures, 66, 67, 70, 83

Inspiration of the Scriptures, 18, 31, 55, 64-66, 68, 70-74, 77, 80, 105, 113

Isaac, 60, 101, 111, 112

I Want to Be a Christian (Packer), 57

Jacob and Esau, 59-61, 67

James, half-brother of Jesus, 19, 127, 128, 136, 137

James, one of the Twelve, 19, 127, 128, 136, 137

Jeroboam, 80

Job, 50, 70, 97, 156

John, one of the Twelve, 55, 136, 137

John the Baptist, 55, 79, 102, 112, 142

Jonah, 61, 126, 154

Joseph, 105, 109, 110, 112, 113

Joshua, 70, 81, 92

Josiah, 80

Kilprect, Kerman, 87

Know Why You Believe (Little), 51

Knox, John, 46

Lewis, C. S., 166

Light of the Gospel, the, 172

Little, Paul, 51

Lloyd-Jones, Martyn, 29

Love, 10, 15-18, 22, 23, 26, 42, 53, 60, 62, 96, 117, 135, 143, 144, 156, 162, 163, 167-169

Luke, 70, 108, 113

Lydia, 155

McCaughey septuplets, 101

McQuilkin, Robertson, 68

Making disciples, 140-142

Manoah, 101

Martyn, Henry, 46

Mary, mother of Jesus, 44, 55, 79, 102-106, 108-113

Matthew, 70

Mere Christianity (Lewis), 166

Morgan, G. Campbell, 26

Morris, Henry, 77

Moses, 36, 53, 58, 61, 71, 73, 78, 107, 126

Naaman, 95

Nebuchadnezzar, 82, 84-86

Neoorthodoxy, 68

Newton, John, 17

Packer, J. I., 56

Paton, John G., 150, 151

Paul, 11, 18, 19, 21, 23, 33, 36-41, 45, 46, 51, 53, 58-60, 64, 70-72, 74, 90, 92, 95, 97, 98, 106, 117, 124-130, 135, 139, 155, 157, 162, 163

Persecution, 17, 125, 150

Peter, 127, 136, 137

Pilate, 120

Pink, A. W., 60

Pluralism, 44

Postmodernism, 63, 69

Prayer, 17, 21, 22, 35-41, 43, 45, 46, 102, 112, 150, 160

Prophecy, 71, 77-81, 83, 88, 104, 105

Quiet Talks with World Winners (Gordon), 145

Rapture, the, 29, 56

Relativism, 9

Repentance, 16, 33, 38, 61, 73, 125, 142, 152, 168

Resurrection of Christ, the, 12, 56, 79, 112 (Chapter 9 passim), 139, 168

Resurrection of God's people, 122, 123

Revival, 9, 16, 29

Samson, 101

Samuel, 36, 102, 112

Sarah, 101, 111

Saul of Tarsus, 46 see also *Paul*

Science and the Bible (Morris), 77

Science Speaks: An Evaluation of Certain Christian Evidences (Stoner), 87

Second Coming, return of Christ, 17-20

Society, Christians' relationship with, 9-11, 15, 24, 40, 41, 127, 149

Solomon, 82

Spencer, Herbert, 71
Spiritual warfare, 10
Spurgeon, C. H., 35, 69, 98, 152
Stephen, 36, 46
Stoner, Peter, 87
Studies in the Sermon on the Mount (Lloyd-Jones), 29
Systematic Theology (Hodge), 52, 55

Timothy, 18, 45, 163
Titanic, the, 146
Today's Gospel: Authentic or Synthetic? (Chantry), 49
Trinity, the, 53-56, 107, 119
Tyre, 81-83

Understanding and Applying the Bible (McQuilkin), 68

Van Dyke, Henry, 98
Virgin birth of Jesus Christ, the, 101 (Chapter 8 passim)

Westminster Confession of Faith, 64
Westminster Shorter Catechism, 59
Whitefield, George, 46
Woman at Sychar, at the well, 144
Wrath of God, 19, 37, 57-59, 62, 97, 119, 123

Zacharias, 102, 111

Other books from The Master's Seminary

What would Jesus say about your Church?

Richard Mayhue   ISBN 1 85792 150X

Starting with the Churches mentioned in Revelation, Mayhue teaches us how to assess the relative strengths and weaknesses of our own churches and delivers a powerful exhortation to implement a process of change.

Includes assessment tools for measuring your church against Jesus' ideal.

How to Interpret the Bible

Richard Mayhue   ISBN 1 85792 2549

A valuable guide to introduce us to a better interpretation of Scripture. Miss-interpretation is one of the major obstacles to church growth as we live in an image centred world that wants short cuts to answers.

"We all need help in approaching the Bible.... This book is not a heavy theological treatise addressed to academics. It is intended for all types of Christian people who are serious about studying the Bible carefully.... I warmly commend it."
Eric Alexander

Coming Soon

Seeking God
How to develop an intimate, spiritual relationship

Richard Mayhue   ISBN 1 85792 5408

Do you have - Spiritual Progress?
              Spiritual Power
              Spiritual Priorities
              Spiritual Passions
              Spiritual Pursuits?

How closely do we walk with, talk with and enjoy God's presence in our lives?

We would love to see our spiritual intimacy with God improve but an intimate relationship is one marked by close association, contact or familiarity. To expand it involves warmth, tenderness, love, transparency, security, vulnerability, strength, commitment, knowledge and understanding.

Is that the sort of relationship you yearn for?

The problem is that our chaotic world is characterised by independence - breeding a brutal, self-seeking attitude devoid of intimacy. This is why marriages crumble, families disintegrate, friendships fail and business turns ugly.

Yet, God beckons us to be intimate with him.

The barbarity of the secular mindset can only be neutralised by spiritual intimacy with a compassionate God. Someone who is utterly trustworthy and whose plans are unable to be put off course. Therefore, our generation's greatest need is to reclaim a sense of intimacy with God, one that will re-shape our souls and re-direct our lives.

This is what you will learn from *Seeking God*